ACCOUNTING THEORY

A CPA Review

ACCOUNTING THEORY

A CPA Review

BENJAMIN NEWMAN
New York University

MARTIN MELLMAN
Bernard M. Baruch School of Business and Public Administration
The City College, City University of New York

JOHN WILEY & SONS, INC.
New York · London · Sydney

PREFACE

In designing this book for the purpose of assisting candidates in the preparation for the CPA Accounting Theory (technically, Theory of Accounts) examination, we have sought to provide the candidate with what we believe he needs most for successful performance on the examination—a fund of major accounting concepts, a knowledge of their essential meaning, and an awareness of their place within the broad framework of generally accepted accounting theory. This objective is consistent, we believe, with the advice contained in the AICPA's booklet *Information for CPA Candidates* that quality and quantity of ideas are what is desired in writing solutions to examination questions and that the central emphasis should be placed on reasoning.

Both as a matter of intrinsic professional value and of examination preparation, it was our aim throughout the book to heighten the student's insight and to facilitate his assimilation and organization of the subject to permit a ready application of basic concepts and ideas in the formulation of solutions to specific questions. Thus Chapter 1 is entirely devoted to an exposition of basic accounting concepts which takes into account the reasons for their general acceptance, their relationships and interdependencies, and their position within the structure of accounting theory. Here and elsewhere, opposing positions and controversial issues are stated and analyzed. In Chapters 2 and 3 the accounting concepts and the generally accepted accounting principles to which they relate are further developed in dealing with revenue recognition and measurement and with cost and cost expiration. Throughout the book, the candidate is led to recognize that the entire framework of accounting theory and its concepts and principles can be viewed as constituting, in effect, the reporting principles and

v

standards designed to achieve fairness in financial reporting. But in Chapter 4, the specific concern is with the technical reporting principles and standards and with the key ideas relating to such topics as informative disclosure, comparability, consistency, contingencies, and conditions of uncertainty. (Several sections of Chapter 4 have been adapted from the book *Auditing: A CPA Review Text* by Benjamin Newman, published by John Wiley and Sons. Grateful acknowledgment is expressed to the author and publisher for permission to use this material.) Ideas and reasoning similarly find their emphasis in Chapter 5 which is devoted to selected accounting and reporting problems including income tax allocation, price-level adjustments, business combinations, and long-term leases.

In thus seeking to provide the candidate with a compact compendium of essential ideas, we recognized that he would still need to refer to his textbooks in financial accounting in order to achieve a comprehensive review of the areas which might be represented on the Accounting Theory examination. Any attempt on our part, however, to extend the scope of the book would have resulted in a voluminous tome duplicating the procedural details and the contents generally of "intermediate" and "advanced" accounting textbooks.

Consistent with its character as a review text, the book develops the subject by an integral combination of textual presentation and solutions to questions drawn from the uniform CPA examinations in Accounting Theory. (We are indebted to the AICPA for the use of these questions.) This framework was adopted out of a strong conviction based upon our teaching, CPA coaching, and other professional experiences that it represents the best method of CPA preparation. Not only does it enable the student to enlarge his knowledge of subject matter, but, at the same time, it provides him with the means of developing skill in communication and in preparing acceptable solutions to examination questions.

The solutions developed in this book are thoroughly comprehensive and include the relevant points for which the CPA candidate might expect to receive credit on the examination. A basic principle of examination taking, which must be constantly borne in mind, is that a solution must be comprehensive if a passing grade is to be attained. The candidate should strive to record as many different relevant ideas as he can express within the time allotted to the question. Similar advice is contained in the booklet *Information for CPA Candidates:* "Top grades go to comprehensive but concise answers. Extremely brief answers, no matter how well directed to the principal points involved, are likely to overlook important points. You should aim for a complete and comprehensive answer."

The points developed in both the textual presentation and the solutions are expressed in a highlighted and concise style so that key ideas and concepts can be quickly picked up by the reader. Captions, subcaptions, key words, and key phrases are frequently used in order to classify the ideas under meaningful groupings and to illuminate the thoughts expressed. Several words of advice and guidance for the candidate may be appropriately offered in this connection: (1) It is unnecessary for the CPA candidate to use these captions or key phrases, although when time is running short he may increase his grade by simply recording such abbreviated phrases if their meaning is clear. (2) To achieve a high passing grade for a particular question, frequently far fewer points or ideas are required than are included in the solutions in this book, but the candidate should constantly strive to make his answers comprehensive, limited only by the allotted time; he should, however, concentrate initially on the principal or major points. (3) Having succinctly but clearly presented a particular point, the candidate should not unduly expand on it, but he should go on to record the next point.

One of the best methods of preparation for the examination is the actual writing of solutions to individual questions. In the course of reading this book, the student may wish to avoid reviewing a given solution and proceed to record his own solution, allowing himself the average time per question of about half an hour. He can then check his solution against that included in the book, comparing particularly the quality and quantity of points and ideas developed. Additional CPA Accounting Theory examination questions and solution guides are included in an appendix and can be used for further review or as additional practice material. The solution guides contain either comprehensive listings of the points to be covered or refer the reader to specific pages in the text which contain the relevant discussions.

Benjamin Newman
Martin Mellman

CONTENTS

ACCOUNTING THEORY

A CPA Review

BASIC ACCOUNTING CONCEPTS

The framework of ideas which make up the body of knowledge of *accounting theory* is the source to which an organization looks in maintaining its accounting records and in preparing financial statements which fairly present the financial condition of the company and the results of its operations. The independent certified public accountant is similarly vitally concerned with the body of generally accepted accounting thought which represents, in effect, the standard which guides him in expressing his independent opinion on the fairness of financial statements which he has examined. The fact that the opinion is rendered by an independent and impartial auditor is the basis for public reliance on his reports. Any exposition of currently accepted accounting theory must therefore deal with a common body of knowledge shared by management, the certified public accountant, and the public. This exposition must also necessarily take into account controversial ideas which may not be currently acceptable for financial reporting purposes.

ORIENTATION

The following broad orientation is intended as an introduction to the discussion of basic accounting concepts to which this chapter is devoted.

1. *Interaction of theory and practice.* The concepts and principles comprising accounting theory are the product of an interaction of professional practice and explicit theoretical formulation. Theory underlies practice and thus serves both as a guide to practice and as a standard for evaluating its acceptability and soundness. But

much of the work in accounting theory has consisted of abstracting and deriving principles from observation and analysis of generally accepted accounting practices.

2. *Significance of practice.* Where theory has thus followed upon practice there has been an implicit assumption that practice would not have become so generally accepted unless it had met crucial historical tests of soundness, practicability, and social usefulness.

3. *Absence of a unified system.* The accounting profession has not as yet developed authoritative and "official" works constituting a unified and integrated system of generally accepted accounting theory. The accounting research bulletins of the AICPA, for example, were directed to those accounting problems and practices with which business and accounting were most urgently involved at the time, many of which related to new economic developments. The new research program of the AICPA has as one of its goals, under the direction of the Accounting Principles Board, the advancement of written expressions of the body of generally accepted accounting principles.

4. *Uniformity in accounting.* A principal objective of the accounting profession is to further the development of generally accepted accounting principles as standards and criteria for judging the suitability of accounting practices. This objective entails narrowing areas of difference and inconsistency in accounting practices but is not intended to obscure essential differences in circumstances that require differences in accounting treatment and the use of alternative accounting methods. Flexibility in this respect is tied in with the concepts of consistency in the use of accounting methods and with disclosure of the principles and practices employed.

5. *Authoritative standing of AICPA pronouncements.* The pronouncements in current force of the American Institute of Certified Public Accountants are presumed to provide the highest authoritative standing with respect to those matters of accounting or auditing with which they deal. The reason for this is that the AICPA is the national society of certified public accountants and represents the public accounting profession in the United States. Although managements and their internal accounting staffs are very much concerned with accounting policies, their orientation is chiefly directed to their individual accounting problems and to the application of generally accepted accounting principles to the conditions of their own companies. In doing so, they regard the CPA profession as the custodian of the body of principles and ascribe to the profession the obligation to develop, expound, refine, and, where necessary, modify these principles.

6. *Opinions of the APB.* The Accounting Principles Board has now the sole authority in the AICPA for the issuance of formal pronouncements, termed *Opinions,* on accounting principles. The authority of the *Opinions* rests upon their general acceptability. However, a special bulletin issued in 1964 by the AICPA's Council, entitled "Disclosure of Departures from Opinion of Accounting Principles Board," requires that material departures from APB Opinions be disclosed in statement footnotes or in the auditor's report. Inasmuch as the accounting research bulletins have been adopted by the APB via Opinion No. 6, their authoritative character is now related to the authority of the APB's *Opinions.* These *Opinions,* however, should not be confused with the accounting research studies published by the Director of Accounting Research of the AICPA as part of the Institute's accounting research program. These studies, which are written by individual authors, do not necessarily reflect the views of the APB and are devoid of authoritative standing. To date nine studies have been issued dealing with the following subjects: (1) Postulates; (2) Cash Flow; (3) Broad Accounting Principles; (4) Reporting of Leases; (5) Business Combinations; (6) Price-level Changes; (7) Inventory of Generally Accepted Accounting Principles; (8) Pension Plans; (9) Income-tax Allocation.

7. *Other authoritative sources.* Since the formal opinions of the Accounting Principles Board and the AICPA's accounting research bulletins do not deal comprehensively with the complete body of accounting principles, when accounting problems arise it is frequently necessary to refer to other authoritative sources. Works of individual authors, the rules and regulations of the Securities and Exchange Commission, and the statements of the American Accounting Association and of other accounting societies are important in this regard. Considerable weight is also placed on generally accepted accounting practices as expressed in published reports.

8. *The Securities and Exchange Commission.* The SEC's rules and regulations on accounting and auditing matters constitute, of course, compelling authoritative guides for the preparation of financial statements required to be filed with it and for the independent accountant's examination and report. Companies and their independent accountants, moreover, are reluctant to report to the SEC on one basis and to stockholders, credit grantors, and others on another basis, especially in view of the requirement that annual reports to stockholders shall disclose material differences between the accounting principles reflected in such reports and those reflected in statements filed with the Commission.

9. *Management's responsibility.* The accounts and the financial statements are the representations and responsibility of management. The auditor's responsibilities relate to his opinion on the statements and to his clear expression, where appropriate, of any qualifications, explanations, or disagreements.

10. *Accounting and the corporate system.* Accounting is essential to any business organization and particularly to corporations, but the success of accounting rests upon the results produced not only for particular interested groups but for society in general. Of special significance are evolutionary changes in the corporate system, absentee ownership, and the factor of ready transferability of stock ownership.

11. *Income statement versus balance sheet.* These evolutionary changes have led to an emphasis on the importance of the income statement and the fair determination of periodic net income. The investor's concern is with net income and earnings per share as indicative of earning capacity, a clear distinction being maintained between recurring and nonrecurring items of profit and loss. This reflects a shift from the previous emphasis upon the balance sheet and the creditor's interest in it as an indication of debt-paying capacity.

12. *Allocation versus valuation.* The central problem in accounting is how to deal in the accounts with costs incurred in one accounting period for the purpose of yielding profits in a future period, that is, how much of an expenditure to assign to current year's operations and how much to carry forward as an asset. Once the proper amount to charge to income has been determined, the residual balance is carried forward on the balance sheet to await future charges to income. The emphasis, therefore, is on the determination of net income rather than on current values. Thus, accounting is often referred to as a process of allocation rather than valuation.

13. *Limitations of financial statements.* Certain limitations relative to the financial statements must be recognized despite the fairness of presentations in conformity with generally accepted accounting principles. The accounts and statements are historical records rather than presentations of current values. Moreover, the periodic statements are tentative installments in the life history of an enterprise and therefore reflect estimates, the impact of transitory factors, and uncertainties as to the future benefits of assets or the outcome of current projects or events. Earning power cannot be properly evaluated without a comparative analysis of profit trends over the years. Financial statements also do not disclose certain matters which can affect operating results, such as management competence and external economic changes in, say, technical processes, markets, and tariffs.

DEFINITION OF ACCOUNTING

A classic definition of accounting formulated by the Committee on Terminology and stated in Accounting Terminology Bulletin No. 1, reads as follows:

Accounting is the art of recording, classifying, and summarizing in a significant manner and in terms of money, transactions and events which are, in part at least, of a financial character, and interpreting the results thereof.

This definition was couched by the Committee in broad language to avoid expressing any undue limitation in the scope of accounting. Certain crucial features, however, which characterize accounting are contained in the definition only by implication. We would want to know, for example, what is meant by the expressions *significant manner* and *interpreting the results*, whose transactions and events are the subject of the art of accounting and for whose benefit the interpretations are made. The following is offered as a more comprehensive definition of accounting in the form of a listing of pertinent elements.

1. *Circumscribing the field of interest; the accounting entity.* Accounting deals with an entity in terms of its economic, business, and financial activities.

2. *Entity activities.* Accounting is concerned with the transactions and events of the entity which are substantially of a financial nature.

3. *Money.* These activities are described in terms of money as a common denominator.

4. *Purpose of accounting.* The function of accounting is to describe these transactions and events in a significant manner and to communicate this information to those interested in understanding the entity.

5. *Classification and recording.* A significant description implies interpretative judgments of the myriad transactions and events of an enterprise. Accounting therefore classifies these transactions and events into significant groupings and records them in books of account.

6. *Method of classification.* A meaningful classification must reflect those aspects and relationships of the entity which are meaningful to those who have, or may have, a material interest in the enterprise. The groupings therefore include the resources held by the entity (that is, assets) and the claims against, and interest in, the entity and its resources (that is, liabilities and ownership interests), as well as any changes in these resources, claims, and interests.

7. *Measurement.* Whether a given event or transaction is to be interpreted as being "ready" for appropriate classification and recording is a matter of judgment and *measurement.* Measurement also entails a judgment as to the dollar amounts which are to be assigned to the resources, claims, interests, etc., and to any changes in these groupings.

8. *Interested parties.* The number of parties who may be interested in an enterprise may be legion. But here, too, accounting groups them into those segments of society which are most likely to have a major interest. These are the entity itself, usually referred to as management, the owners (stockholders), creditors, governmental agencies, and, in general, any other groups such as customers who may have significant dealings with the enterprise.

9. *Form of presentation.* Accounting summarizes and interprets the results of the entity's activities. Such summarization and interpretation may involve segments of the entity's activities such as costing of products. It is, however, the summarization and interpretation of the *overall* results of the activities of the entity as a *whole* which is the chief function of accounting in serving the needs of the aforementioned interested parties. This is frequently referred to as financial accounting, financial reporting, or general-purpose reporting. The presentation is in the form of financial statements which consist, for most types of enterprises, of a balance sheet to present the financial condition as of a given date, and a statement of income (and a statement of retained earnings for a corporation, or statement of capital for an individual proprietorship or partnership) to portray the results of operations for a period ended that date.

10. *Art or science.* The Committee on Terminology refers to accounting as an art in order to emphasize the creative skill and ability with which the accountant applies his knowledge to particular problems. But the Committee suggests that accounting includes the elements of a science insofar as it deals with "ordered classifications" as a framework within which transactions and events are fitted.

11. *Body of principles.* This framework may be described as a body of concepts, principles, and rules which constitutes a mechanism for understanding and portraying the economic activities of an entity.

THE NATURE OF THE ACCOUNTING ENTITY

The entity which accounting portrays may be a corporation, a partnership, or an individual proprietorship. It may be conducted for profit or nonprofit purposes. It may be public or private. The entity may be a recognized legal unit like a corporation or it may be informal and untraditional like a personal venture or, say, a household. Once the entity has been identified as that to which the accounting function is to be directed, it becomes the accounting entity, that is, a body or organism that is regarded as having a real and separate existence.

As thus conceived, the accounting entity seems to be a fiction since in many instances the economic unit which has been selected as the subject to be accounted for may not enjoy legal status as a separate "person." Actually, there is nothing fictional about the accounting entity. An accounting entity is created only when there is a need for its creation. It originates when an economic unit has been identified and there is a need to understand its economic and financial activities *as a unit*. The selection of the entity to be accounted for is determined not by the system of accounting but by the external social, economic, and legal environment and its practical requirements. The accounting entity is therefore a selected economic unit and this concept can be formally expressed as follows:

Any economic unit which has been selected as the subject to be accounted for (that is, as the accounting entity) is to be viewed, in the accounting process, as a real entity, existing in its own right separate and distinct from other entities which have dealings with it.

If an individual owns and operates several businesses as individual proprietorships, we can create an accounting entity for each business, for any number in any combination, or for all combined. Indeed, the individual himself can be treated as an accounting entity to embrace all his economic and financial activities, both business and personal.

PROPRIETARY, ENTITY, AND FUNDS THEORIES
REGARDING THE SEPARATE ENTITY

Granted that the accounting entity is an economic unit, there nevertheless exist various ways of interpreting its character as a separate entity. The accounting for the entity may depend on the viewpoint adopted. Those who take the position that the entity is to be viewed as completely separate and apart from its owners, who would then take on the status akin to creditors, are said to espouse the *entity theory*. Others who identify the entity's activities with the owners of the enterprise adopt what is called the *proprietary theory*. The *funds theory* views the entity as a medium for holding assets in trust. These views are sometimes referred to as concepts.

Question—May 1959 (8)

Three theories of accounting equities are: (1) the proprietary theory (2) the entity theory, and (3) the funds theory.

(a) Describe briefly each of these theories.

(b) State your reasons for emphasizing the application of one of these theories to each of the following: (i) single proprietorship; (ii) partnership; (iii) financial institutions (banks); (iv) consolidated statements; (v) estate accounting.

Solution

Proprietary Theory

1. *General perspective.* According to this theory the entity belongs to the owners and is so viewed by them, and the accounting is expected to emphasize and reflect this identification of the enterprise with the proprietor's interests and outlook.

2. *Assets.* The assets are viewed as belonging to the owners and not to the entity.

3. *Liabilities.* The liabilities are considered to be obligations of the proprietors.

4. *Net worth.* The capital of the entity is viewed as belonging to the owners. It is calculated as the amount of assets which would remain for the owners on the assumption that all creditors had been paid. The balance sheet presentation in the form of "assets minus liabilities equals capital" is clearly expressive of the proprietary concept. But it should be understood that the use of this form, which is frequently followed in practice, does not signify the adoption of the proprietary concept. It is the entity concept which underlies generally accepted accounting.

5. *Earnings.* The proprietary approach views the income-producing activities of the entity as being carried on by the proprietors and for their benefit. The following are some of the consequences of this concept.

(a) Earnings are the result of individual transactions, but are viewed from the standpoint of increases in the net worth of the enterprise not attributable to net additional investments.

(b) The proprietors do not have only a claim to the income;

it is viewed as actually belonging to them, as *their* income. In the case of corporations, the dissemination of figures of per-share earnings suggests the proprietary outlook.

(c) In measuring their personal earnings, investors may look beyond the entity's income or net worth and focus their attention on the value of their investment. For example, stockholders will figure their earnings by the increase in the value of their stockholdings. The recorded income of the entity may be considered only one of the factors affecting this value. Other factors, not recognized by the entity but important to the investor who assumes the proprietary role, may be unrealized income, unrecorded increases in asset values, and prospective earnings.

6. *Life of entity.* The entity's existence is viewed as dependent on the will of the owners. Consequently, the entity's life is regarded as contingent. A liquidation status is implicit in this view. The owners will tend to measure the value of their investment on the assumption that the enterprise can be liquidated by them at any time.

7. *Acceptability.* The proprietary concept enjoyed a larger measure of support in earlier years when noncorporate forms of business organizations predominated in which the owners, doing business as proprietorships or partnerships, managed and controlled the entity with which they were identified in law and in fact. Although accounting does not recognize the proprietary theory and there are few accountants who would be willing to apply it fully with all of the consequences, the concept continues to exert a subtle influence in certain areas, of which some are in controversy. Some examples are: balance sheet presentation and description of capital accounts; objections to the use of any surplus reserve accounts as suggestive of the availability for dividends of the unreserved surplus; and, more importantly, attacks on the cost basis of accounting and advocacy of current values in its stead.

Entity Theory

1. *General perspective.* If the entity concept is followed, the accounting entity is viewed as if it had a real and separate existence completely distinct from the owners or investors, and certainly from the creditors.

2. *Assets.* The assets are regarded as belonging to the entity, whether originating with creditors or investors.

3. *Liabilities.* The liabilities are viewed as the debts of the entity itself, even though, in the case of a proprietorship or partnership,

creditors may look to the owners' personal assets for satisfaction of their claims. The liabilities are perceived as having equitable claims against the entity and its assets.

4. *Net worth.* The capital of the entity is regarded somewhat in the same light as liabilities and represents an equity interest in the entity of the owners or investors. To be sure, the accounting presentation distinguishes between the claims of creditors and the claims of investors and owners. The balance sheet presentation which corresponds to the entity concept is in the form of "assets equals equities," with equity interests classified into liabilities and capital. In practice, many balance sheets show both the capital and liability accounts under a joint classification entitled *liabilities* or *equities.*

5. *Earnings.* The income-producing activities of the entity are viewed as being engaged in by the entity itself, for its own benefit and well-being just as if it were a person and capable of self-determination. Its decision-making power, of course, is exercised through those who manage it and act, collectively and for this purpose, as the alter ego of the entity. The following are some of the consequences which result from these assumptions:

(a) Assets contributed to the entity by the "owners" create a corresponding "obligation" to the donors and are valued on the same basis as a purchase. The cost of assets is cost *to the entity* and assets are stated at cost. Assets purchased or contributed "belong" to the entity and not to the investors.

(b) Earnings result from the enterprise's own activities and not from dealings with the owners, such as in capital stock transactions or investments or drawings of partners. The value of the total entity (for example, what the business can be sold for) is meaningless to the enterprise itself. Thus goodwill ascribed to the company does not enter into its earnings calculations and does not serve as an asset unless purchased by it.

(c) Costs incurred in realizing income are the costs incurred by the entity itself.

(d) The earnings of the enterprise result from individual transactions and are accounted for on that basis. They are not measured by increases, from period to period, in net assets or net worth viewed as a whole.

(e) Because owners and creditors are both regarded as having an equitable interest in the entity, it might be thought that since dividends are treated as a distribution of income to stockholders, interest on loans and income taxes should be similarly presented as distributions of income. But the entity theory does not take this extreme position in practice, interest and taxes being regarded as expenses. This reflects a practical recognition of the difference in status of creditors and owners.

6. *Life of entity.* As an entity enjoying a separate existence, it may be viewed as a going concern having an indefinite life. When investors adopt this view, they will measure the value of their investment on the basis of their expectations of the future progress of the enterprise.

7. *Acceptability.* The entity theory is the one currently held as being in accordance with generally accepted accounting. Its acceptance has been reinforced by the growth of corporate organization. The corporation is itself a legal entity distinct from its stockholder-owners. This separation is accentuated by the growth of absentee ownership resulting from the complexity and size of business organizations and the wide dispersion of stock ownership. The accounting entity has thereby taken on a public character so that, while separate from owners and creditors alike, it is expected to provide accounting data which show how it has utilized its resources and what accountabilities it has to outside parties. Although the concept is most clearly grasped when applied to corporations, it is also the basis of accounting for proprietorships, partnerships, and other forms of business organizations.

Funds Theory

1. *General perspective.* This approach views the entity as a medium for holding assets in trust in accordance with the purposes and restrictions which governed the creation of the fund or entity. This concept may be applied to the entire entity, to specific assets, or to designated activities. The fund concept is particularly applicable to the accounting for governmental bodies, for estates and trusts, and for nonprofit organizations in general. Commercial enterprises may establish a fund for a specific purpose but this would not be incompatible with accounting for the entire company on the basis of the entity theory.

2. *Assets.* The emphasis is on the custody of fund assets, on changes in those assets, and in their use for the designated purposes, rather than on income-producing operations.

3. *Liabilities.* Debts of the entity or fund are presented as liabilities in the same way as in the entity or proprietary theory, but creditors are not viewed either as having an equitable interest in the fund or as looking to the owners as obligors.

4. *Net worth.* The net worth of the entity or fund is viewed in

two ways: first, as corresponding to the net assets (that is, assets less liabilities) to be accounted for under the fund arrangement, and second, as descriptive of the purpose for which the fund was created and of the restrictions which govern its use. The balance sheet form may correspond to that used to suggest either the entity or proprietary theory, but the capital account is given a title such as "principal-general fund," "principal-water works fund" or "reserve for bond sinking fund" to indicate the activity, purpose, or restriction.

5. *Earnings.* The focus is directly on the proper investment and use of funds in accordance with specified restrictions. The income derived from the fund assets is accorded a secondary status as being simply a consequence of the proper and restricted use of the assets.

6. *Life of entity.* The funds theory implies an existence for the entity whose duration is limited by the restrictions and purposes which prompted its original creation. A fund for building construction will expire upon the completion of the activity; an estate or trust will terminate at the time specified in the will or agreement. Some fund entities, like a municipality or charitable institution, may have an indefinite life.

7. *Acceptability.* The fund theory is most appropriate for entities like estates, governmental agencies, and nonprofit organizations whose chief concentration is on the custody and use of assets for special restricted purposes.

Application of Theories

1. *Single proprietorship.* The proprietary theory is most easily understood when applied to a proprietorship because of the close identification of the owner with the business unit, his personal liability to creditors, his uninhibited claim to the income, and his control over the business.

2. *Partnership.* A partnership has features which suggest either the proprietary or the entity concepts. The fact that there are several owners whose outlook and interests may vary compels an emphasis on the separate entity notion. To satisfy their claims the creditors must look first to partnership assets which are owned by the partnership as a unit. If the assets are insufficient, creditors can then turn to the assets of individual partners which are, however, subject to the prior claim of partners' personal creditors. But the personal liability of partners and their close association with the entity convey a proprietary emphasis.

3. *Banks and other financial institutions.* To even a greater degree than for corporations engaged in manufacturing or merchandising,

these institutions are invested with a public interest. Depositors and other creditors may have a more vital stake in the entity than the stockholders. The applicability of the entity theory is most clear.

4. *Consolidated statements.* The consolidated entity may be viewed as:

(a) a separate economic unit encompassing the individual units of parent and subsidiary companies, reflecting the entity concept;

(b) being the parent company which has absorbed subordinate units, reflecting the proprietary concept;

(c) a consolidated statement of funds, the assets of the subsidiaries and parent being viewed as funds.

5. *Estate accounting.* The funds theory is most directly applicable to estates. The focus in accounting for the estate as an entity is on the conservation, custody, and changes of the assets strictly within the specified limitations and restrictions as to their use and disposition. The effects of changes in assets are distinguished in accordance with the accountabilities to income and principal beneficiaries.

SINGLE SET OF FINANCIAL STATEMENTS

Accounting theory rests upon the fact that only one set of financial statements is conventionally issued for general-reporting purposes. These statements, which usually consist of a balance sheet, a statement of income, and a statement of retained earnings (or statement of capital for a proprietorship or partnership), are referred to as all-purpose or general-purpose statements. Long-form reports of independent accountants that are prepared for management purposes and, sometimes, for credit grantors, may contain additional information and supplementary supporting schedules which support the basic statements. But whether the report is long-form or short-form, the basic statements are the same in all material respects.

How can one set of statements provide the accounting data and their necessary interpretation for such diverse interests as management, creditors, and investors and still maintain an internal consistency when there may be conflicting needs among the groups and even within each group? The answer is that the general-purpose statements and the accounting theory which they reflect represent an endeavor to achieve a composite portrayal of the entity as a whole which is designed to provide selectively for certain major needs which the several groups have in common or may be more urgently possessed by one without detriment to the others.

It is obvious that a composite presentation involves some compromise and sacrifice. For example, credit grantors might wish to receive financial statements prepared on the assumption that the entity might shortly have to be liquidated so that they may know how secure their loan would be under such circumstance. Management, however, expects that the statements will reflect the character of the enterprise as a going concern and must frequently make decisions which involve uncertainties and conjecture. The investor may be interested in statements which show *both* the liquidation status of the organization (to ascertain recoverability of investment upon such an occurrence) and the going concern condition as well as estimates of future earnings (as an aid in deciding whether to hold, buy, or sell stock in the company). Yet, assuming the availability of all of this information, the data cannot be consistently presented in one set of statements because one basis assumes the existence of circumstances not present on another basis.

The total system of accounting theory is designed to deal with the problem of providing through a single accounting mechanism and a single set of statements a presentation of the financial condition and operations of an enterprise which can be regarded as a unified and fair portrayal for the benefit and use of all interested persons. This concept can be formally expressed as follows:

The activities of an entity are summarized in a single set of related financial statements in which the several statements reflect consistent interpretation and treatment of the same underlying data and combine to form a unified presentation.

The requirement with respect to consistency among the statements should not be confused with the idea of consistency from period to period in the application of accounting principles. It means that an established interpretation of data in one financial statement must be consistently followed, relative to the same underlying data, in another statement. An example of this is the rule stated in ARB No. 43, Chapter 9b, "Depreciation on Appreciation," and reaffirmed in APB Opinion No. 6. If depreciable assets are written up (although this practice is generally unacceptable) and so reflected on the balance sheet, the income statement must correspondingly show the depreciation on the appreciated assets.

The notion regarding unified presentation ensures significant connections among statements and a clear portrayal of their relatedness. Thus the statement of income ties in with the statement of retained earnings, and the latter with the balance sheet. Supporting schedules in turn may lead into specific accounts on the balance sheet or statement of income, whereas a statement of application of funds is integrally related to both balance sheet and income statement.

A COMMON BODY OF PRINCIPLES

Why has accounting adopted the concept of a single set of financial statements when it could have permitted the issuance of pluralistic statements—a wide variety of statements, each set of which would be oriented to different groups and perspectives? In this way each person or group could pick and choose from the common fount the particular presentation which serves his individual need. The following are the reasons for adherence to the concept which prescribes a single set of related statements and, in general, to the conception of a common body of generally accepted accounting principles which underlie the statements for general-reporting purposes.

1. *Common frame of reference.* Although it may contain imperfections and does not fulfill all possible requirements, the body of generally accepted accounting principles does provide a presentation which constitutes a clearly identifiable and common frame of reference. Business decisions involve comparisons of operations and financial condition of the entity from period to period and of one enterprise with another in the same or different industry. It would be impossible for such decisions to be made unless comparability were made possible by the existence of a commonly understood body of generally accepted accounting principles.

2. *Fair presentation.* Although other systems of accounting theory may yield different and even useful results, the currently accepted system is designed to achieve a fair presentation of the entity's financial position and activities for the joint benefit of all interested parties.

The complexities of the accounting entity and of the social and economic environment within which it functions make it impossible for any one system of accounting to fully encompass these complexities and to draw into one universal presentation the many-faceted perspectives from which the entity may be viewed. Within this unavoidable limitation, financial statements prepared in conformity with generally accepted accounting principles are fair presentations, provide useful and significant information, and meet the critical pragmatic test of their successful use in the everyday world of business and social affairs.

3. *A focal point.* The single set of statements and the common

body of accounting principles provide a focal and stable point from which divergent lines may be drawn when management or other groups experience a special need to modify the basic system. The basic statements may serve, for example, as a starting point in negotiations between the buyer and seller of a business or for supplementary reports which reflect price-level changes.

4. *Pluralistic statements and misleading inferences.* If a multivariety of statements were issued for public use, each being independent of the others and each purporting to tell the "truth" about the entity from a particular perspective, this pluralism could only result in misleading inferences and in confusion. Only professional accountants or individuals close to the entity and having an extremely high degree of training and sophistication could understand and assimilate such an abundance of discrete and often inconsistent data. Equally significant is the opportunity which would exist for unscrupulous manipulation starting with the arbitrary selection of emphases in constructing the statements and extending to the arbitrary selection of the statements to be issued or published.

5. *Practicability.* Even if pluralistic statements did not lead to confusion, it would still not be practicable for them to replace the single set of statements as presently conceived. Uniform and generally accepted accounting principles would have to be developed for each type of statement. The years of tradition, practice, theory construction, and the pragmatic tests of theory which have gone into the refinement of the body of currently accepted principles would have to be duplicated to some extent for each of the many different bodies of theory which would underlie the many different types of statements.

6. *The idea of unity.* The businessman—the investor, the creditor, the customer—seeks regularity, stability, and a common ground for understanding and, hence, tends to regard the multiple realities and truths regarding the entity as consisting of one truth or one reality or some consistent combination which can be grasped as a unity. It is this practical demand for a unified portrayal which makes impracticable the issuance of multivariety statements.

OVERALL SUMMARIZATION

An entity may be analyzed into its component parts or functions in many different ways. An entity may be composed of a number of entities. A consolidated entity includes subsidiary corporations. A single corporation may be made up of a number of operating divisions. A manufacturing enterprise carries on manufacturing, selling, and administrative functions. The products produced and sold may be selected as the subject of analysis.

The concept of a single set of statements does not necessarily restrict the extent of detail to be included in the financial statements nor does it preclude the reporting on the separate activities of subsidiary companies, divisions, functions, products, or any other chosen classification. Financial reporting, however, presents only the overall results of the activities of the entity taken as a whole in accordance with a basic accounting concept which may be worded as follows:

The financial statements are summarizations of the overall results of the activities of an entity taken as a whole.

This concept recognizes that it is the whole entity with which we are concerned rather than with its parts, and that the whole is something different than simply the sum of the parts. There is also the practical consideration that it would be exceedingly difficult to achieve general agreement either as to the component parts which should be selected for reporting purposes or the basis on which they would be presented. Moreover, the very mass of data and details could be confusing to the general reader. These considerations, however, do not preclude a company from furnishing in a long-form report more detailed information regarding component segments and other data.

FORM AND CONTENT OF STATEMENTS

Given the concept that the statements are overall summarizations, how does accounting determine how to summarize and present the overall results of an entity's activities in a manner which will have both significance and uniform meaning for the readers of the financial statements?

Accounting entities engage in myriads of transactions and there are many different types of entities ranging from commercial enterprises to nonprofit organizations and governmental units. But all entities have this in common—that they are man-made and are created for a purpose. An entity undertakes activities to achieve the objectives for which it was created. Its activities therefore necessarily involve the effort expended to achieve the objectives, and the accomplishments or the extent to which the objectives have been achieved. Effort expended is measured in accounting by the resources (that is, assets) given up while accomplishment is reflected in the revenue and income earned. Furthermore, accounting reports on the financial condition of an entity at a given point in time so that we may know the resources which remain with the entity for similarly carrying on in the future, the claims which outside parties have against these resources and, in general, the capability of the entity for continuing its efforts and for meeting its obligations.

In summary, the accounting concept which determines the form and content of the financial statements may be stated as follows:

The financial statements summarize the overall results of an entity's activities by means of classifications and groupings of such classifications designed to show: (1) for a given period, the nature of the accomplishments (revenue) of the entity, the resources (assets) given up in the process, and the net results (net income or loss); and (2) as of the end of the period, the resources (assets) which remain, the uses to which they have been committed, the nature of claims (liabilities) against them and the conditions imposed by these claims.

OBJECTIVITY IN ACCOUNTING

The concept of objectivity is fundamental to accounting. Objectivity is both a state of mind and a course of action. An accounting judgment is not objective unless it is solidly supported by facts. The willingness to express a judgment without such firm grounds is clear evidence of a state of mind which is not objective, however impartial the accountant may believe himself to be. The concept of objectivity in accounting therefore entails a course of action to seek out all the relevant facts upon which a sound judgment may be based. The concept may be succinctly stated as follows:

The data which enter into the accounting process are based upon objective, verifiable evidence.

The following should serve to clarify further the meaning of objectivity.

1. *State of mind.* Objectivity is dynamic even as to the state of mind of the accountant. He must not only believe that he is objective but must also maintain a state of constant vigilance and self-scrutiny to ensure that there is no subtle infiltration of subjective influences.

2. *The nature of subjectivity.* Subjectivity is the opposite of objectivity. Individuality and uniqueness are the essence of subjectivity. A subjective interpretation is an individual interpretation and the conclusions so drawn are colored by the person's unique make-up,

by his individual capabilities and limitations, and even by bias which may be deliberate or unintentional. The environment which accounting seeks to describe can be said to be viewed subjectively if the data upon which accounting judgments are made are insufficient or indefinite and therefore conducive to speculation and arbitrary interpretation.

3. *Common agreement.* Objectivity, on the other hand, connotes generality, common agreement, and universal understanding. Objectivity in accounting entails a continuous mental comparison by the accountant of his judgment with what he believes would be the general judgment of other disinterested parties including other accountants. The more susceptible a fact is to common agreement as to its nature and significance, the more objective is it deemed to be and the more acceptable as a basis for drawing inferences and conclusions.

4. *Sufficiency of facts.* The greater the number of facts which support a judgment, the closer does the accountant come to a fruitful presentation of the realities which it aims to portray.

5. *Inference and interpretation.* It is also recognized that different interpretations and inferences may be made from the same set of facts, however objective these facts may seem to be. Objectivity therefore demands that in making any inferences and interpretations from these facts, the accountant must carefully consider the reasonableness and logic of such conclusions and again judge whether there would be substantial agreement among other impartial persons as to their validity.

6. *Relativity.* Objectivity is a relative concept. Any facts and any judgments however objective they may appear to be can be challenged by some on the ground that they reflect some degree of subjectivity. Even though it is theoretically an ideal, objectivity is achieved in accounting as a practical matter when accounting strives, as it does, to attain that ideal.

7. *Objective, verifiable evidence.* The concept of verifiability is implicit in the idea of objectivity. This is most evident in the work of the independent auditor, but the existence and availability of objective, verifiable evidence are an indispensable part of the accounting function in general.

OBJECTIVE, VERIFIABLE EVIDENCE

Something is evidence in accounting if it tends to verify the reality of an event or the soundness of a judgment, both of which may have accounting consequences. Evidence is verifiable if it is readily available for examination and evaluation and its authenticity can be verified. It is objective to the extent that it is definite, clear-cut, and independent of the subjective behavior of those most concerned with the event to which it is related. The following is a clarification of some significant aspects of objective, verifiable evidence and of the reasons for its importance as an accounting concept.

1. *A foundation.* It provides a foundation for objectivity in accounting because it is factual in nature and therefore conducive to substantial agreement among disinterested persons as to the nature and significance of the facts and realities represented.

2. *Verification of subjective facts.* The opinions, intentions, and objectives of management or other parties are important facts in the environment of accounting and frequently determine accounting treatment, but they have subjective features. An opinion may be expressed, for example, by the credit manager of a company as to the allowance for bad debts which should be provided. The opinion is evidence but it is not objective. The accountant would give the opinion a certain weight but, before recording the appropriate entry, would first review objective evidence such as credit reports, an aged schedule of receivables, and relevant correspondence.

3. *A basis for sound judgments.* Accounting may be affected by judgments on a variety of matters such as the useful life of depreciable property, obsolescence of merchandise, future warranty costs applicable to current year's sales, or valuation of assets received in exchange for capital stock. The existence and availability of objective evidence provide management itself with a basis for making sound judgments. The lack of such evidence would serve to disclose the essential subjectivity of a judgment.

4. *Arms-length transactions.* Accounting assumes that objectivity will govern the transactions between parties. Arms-length transactions are more apt to give rise to objective, verifiable evidence in support of the transaction and its accounting.

5. *Analysis.* Before transactions can be recorded they must be analyzed in order to understand their true significance. A lease arrangement may be one in form only but, after analysis of the lease provisions and other objective evidence, it may be determined that it is in substance an installment purchase. What appears to be a sale may actually be a consignment shipment. Objective evidence enables the accountant to analyze a transaction or event so that its nature may be precisely determined, thereby assuring the accuracy of accounting entries.

6. *Verification by the independent public accountant.* Although accounting by its nature is objective, assurance that it is so for any given accounting entity is provided by the report and opinion submitted by the independent public accountant. His report and opinion will be affected by the existence and availability of objective evidence which tends to confirm the representations of management.

CERTAINTY AND UNCERTAINTY

Objectivity implies certainty and definiteness. Accounting therefore seeks to record what is definite and certain and accepts indefiniteness and uncertainty cautiously and reluctantly and only when compelled to do so by the inherent character of the activities and environment of the accounting entity.

A transaction or other event is said to be definite if it is so clearly discernible and precisely defined as to be unmistakable. If a company arranges for a bank loan, signs a note, and receives the proceeds, then the transaction is definite and it is unmistakable that a liability exists. A purchase order is received from a customer and the order is accepted. It is definite that a commitment exists but this, by itself, does not establish whether a sale will actually take place and is to be recorded in the accounts. In general, accounting will equate definiteness and certainty with fully completed transactions.

Many of the events with which accounting must deal owe their indefiniteness to the fact that they relate to the future and their outcome therefore is not certain. Events take place in time, and the probability of their occurrence may be better expressed by the ideas of certainty and uncertainty or probability rather than definiteness and indefiniteness. Accounting is an historical description of the past and present. But there are elements of the future in both the past and present which cannot be escaped. The cost of machinery acquired during the year is certain, but the depreciation charged for the period and the amount of the remaining asset balance will depend on estimates of its future useful life. The price paid for merchandise is known, but the valuation of inventory at the balance sheet date will be affected by a judgment concerning future salability and sales price. There may be future expenses, like warranty costs, which are ascribable to past operations and must be currently recorded. Current valuations of research and development costs incurred in the past will depend on judgment regarding their value in future operations. The amount at which accounts receivable are stated on the balance sheet will depend on estimates as to future bad debt losses, although the receivables originated in the past and their balances are stated as of the present. Accounting must necessarily take the future into consideration.

DEALING WITH UNCERTAINTY

The following is an outline of the major approaches which accounting brings to the problem of dealing with uncertainty and of providing, to the extent it can, an effective basis for the exercise of judgment.

1. *The framework of theory.* The concepts and principles which enter into the framework of accounting theory provide objective standards by their general acceptance. Thus the realization principle flatly states that income is not recognized until actually realized by consummated transactions.

2. *Conservatism.* The concept of conservatism provides a major guide, when doubt or uncertainty is present, as to such matters as the write-off of long-term assets, valuation of inventories, and the current recording of future losses which stem from present conditions.

3. *Disclosure.* When a sound judgment as to the probability of a contingency materializing cannot be made and an accounting entry that would otherwise have been appropriate cannot be recorded, the principle of full disclosure comes into play. The known data and the fact of the contingency will be disclosed in the financial statements by a footnote.

4. *Objective basis for estimates.* Even though estimates must be made, it is expected that such judgments will be based, to the extent possible, on known and objective facts related to the past or present. The estimate of future bad debts, for example, will be based on past experience, analysis of the accounts receivable, and the like.

5. *Accounting methods.* The very variety of accounting methods available to the accountant is useful not only in the application of broad principles to individual situations but also in the exercise of judgment in areas of uncertainty. Thus the acceptability of declining-balance, straight-line, units-of-production, and other depreciation methods allows the accountant to choose that method which best enables him to cope with the degree of uncertainty in a given situation concerning the useful life of the depreciable assets.

6. *Systematic procedures.* The well-known accounting methods, such as declining-balance depreciation or Fifo method of costing

inventories, are systematic—that is, they have a definite design which can be carried out methodically and uniformly. Even though there may be some indefiniteness as to the subject matter to which the accounting method is applicable—for example, the useful life of property—at least an accounting procedure which is systematic produces results which are explicit and definitely identifiable.

7. *Post-balance sheet review.* A review of transactions occurring between the balance sheet date and the date the financial statements are prepared may shed additional light on the status of uncompleted transactions or events.

IMPUTED COSTS

Consistent with its emphasis upon objectivity and certainty, accounting eschews the concept of imputation when coupled with supposition. The term *imputation* means the act of ascribing to something an element which is not clearly a part of it. When overhead or joint costs, for example, are assigned or allocated to specific products, the amount allocated to any given product may be said to be imputed to it. A cost *directly* associated with a product is *clearly* a part of the cost of that product and is not referred to as *imputed*. Because overhead costs are in fact definite costs and clearly exist, there is nothing hypothetical or conjectural about such allocation. The chief problem is to find some equitable and objective basis for allocation. Because of this, such terms as *allocation* or *assignment* of costs are used rather than *imputation* and such procedures are regarded as being fully legitimate.

There are many examples, however, of imputation which are not acceptable to accounting because they involve supposition and conjecture. Economists, for example, view the net income of a proprietorship as consisting of the management "salary" of the proprietor, interest on capital invested in the business, and "pure" profit. They would have accounting present such "salary" and "interest" as expenses in the statement of income so that the final profit would represent the "pure" economic profit. Accounting does not recognize these imputed expenses. There would be such difficulties in arriving at an objective measurement of the amount at which salaries and interest should be stated that the door would be open to subjective and arbitrary judgment. But more importantly, expenses were not actually incurred. The economic view conceives of these expenses as costs on the theory, for example, that the proprietor has forgone the opportunity to earn interest on his capital which could have been otherwise invested.   These imputed costs are therefore also referred to as *opportunity costs.*

Accounting does not look upon such imputed costs as real.   Accounting describes what exists and not what could have happened under hypothetical conditions.   Indeed, to pursue the example further, if the proprietor had not invested in the business the accounting entity itself would be nonexistent.

Accounting sees nothing wrong in preparing special statements reflecting such imputed costs when they may be useful for managerial planning, but the entire concept is excluded from the framework of generally accepted accounting theory and general-purpose reporting.

INFERENCE AND INTERPRETATION

It is the task of accounting to depict events objectively, but the presentation must also reveal their significance.   This is illustrated by the accounting concept which, in determining the form and content of financial statements, calls for a showing as to the nature of the accomplishments, the resources, the uses to which assets have been committed, claims against the assets, etc.   The significance of events or facts is not always self-evident and it is frequently necessary to interpret data.   The danger in drawing inferences from given data is that the conclusions may not follow, as a matter of logical necessity, from the data or may involve assumptions which have not been established as being sound.   It must also be recognized that the same set of facts may be interpreted differently depending upon the viewpoint of the analyst.

Where an event is subject to different interpretations regarding its economic significance, accounting favors that interpretation which is most consistent with the concept of objectivity.   A current problem in accounting—the accounting for long-term leases—can serve as an illustration.

If a lease arrangement is in substance an installment purchase and this is evidenced by objective facts, accounting will look beyond the legal form and account for the transaction as a purchase, showing the asset and liability and treating the periodic rentals as payment of interest and amortization of the "mortgage."   There are many accountants who contend that all long-term leases should be treated essentially as the purchase of a property right to be accounted for on a basis somewhat similar to the cases in which the lease is in substance a purchase. This interpretation is not acceptable to accounting for the reasons previously mentioned—the objective facts are that the arrangement is a rental of property and there are no objective facts which point to the contrary; it is generally viewed by the contracting parties as a lease agreement; assumptions would have to be made if interpreted as a purchase, but such assumptions and the conjecture which they may entail are not as manifest when the agreement is seen as a standard lease; and finally, leases have always been an objective and identifiable part of the economic environment and the standard view of their significance has been reinforced by convention and tradition.

VALUE, MEASUREMENT, AND MONEY

As used in accounting, the term *value* connotes economic utility. *Measurement* is the process of expressing value in quantitative terms, but the word is most often used with respect to income and expense accounts. *Valuation* has substantially the same meaning as *measurement*, but it is applied mainly to balance sheet accounts and paticularly to assets.

Accounting expresses values in terms of money. It would be difficult, if not impossible, to use any other medium of measurement. Economic transactions are in fact described and consummated on a money basis. Moreover, it represents a standard by which the heterogeneous items reflected in the financial statements may assume a homogeneous form. It is a common denominator which has the attribute of objectivity. It is also public in character and universally understandable and therefore essential for the public use of financial statements.

FIXED MONETARY STANDARD

Accounting theory is affected by the way the monetary standard itself is viewed. One view holds that recorded values should be adjusted periodically to reflect changes in the value of money; that is, price-level changes. It is well known that the purchasing power of the dollar does not remain constant and its value has in fact fluctuated over the years. However, accounting has been unwilling to introduce into the accounts modifications of values in order to reflect changes in the value of the monetary standard. The view which conforms with generally accepted accounting principles holds to the concept that:

Values in accounting are expressed in terms of money as a fixed and constant standard.

This concept, which is one of several making up the generally accepted historical cost basis of accounting, is often taken to signify adherence to an assumption that the dollar (or other monetary unit) is a stable unit and that its purchasing power, or value, does not change. But accounting does not at all assume something which is contrary to fact. The proposition simply chooses to ignore changing values of the monetary unit. The following are some of the important reasons for the adherence by accounting to the concept of a fixed monetary standard and to historical cost accounting.

1. *Objectivity.* Values expressed in terms of the money amounts entering into actual exchanges are objective and supportable by objective, verifiable evidence.

2. *Focal point.* Such values constitute a focal and stable frame of reference which provides a point of departure if it is desired to prepare supplementary statements on a price-level basis.

3. *Supplementary statements and experimentation.* Management may prepare if it wishes supplementary statements which show the effects of increasing price levels.

4. *Confusion.* Price-level accounting would entail such a radical change in the entire structure of accounting theory as to lead to public confusion and misunderstanding of financial statements.

5. *Practicability.* Such a change in the structure of accounting would involve the unusual restatement of accounts of all entities to a current-value basis and continuous adjustments thereafter as the purchasing power of the dollar fluctuates. Such current restatement of values and subsequent modifications thereof must be supported by objective standards and must be universally carried out. The very magnitude of such an operation, assuming objective standards could be agreed upon, makes it presently impracticable.

6. *Necessity.* Inflation has not as yet advanced so far that it impairs the significance of costs stated in original dollars.

TYPES OF VALUE

Various bases exist on which values for accounting data might conceivably be stated. Values in accounting are based largely on cost in accordance with the concept of objectivity. In order to understand the rationale which underlies the accounting concept of value, it is important to clarify the meaning of various terms used in accounting which denote various types of value or are related to the concept of value.

1. *Value in exchange.* The economic activities of an accounting entity consist mainly of transactions which involve exchanges of goods or services. Value in exchange is reflected in the *price* paid or received for such goods or services. *Measured consideration, price aggregate,* or *bargained price* are terms sometimes used to signify price or to emphasize some aspect of it. *Measured consideration* is used synonymously with *price aggregate,* which means the total price (that is, unit price times quantity) set in a transaction. *Bargained price* suggests that the price was determined by the "market," objectively and at arms-length. Value in exchange, as thus objectively arrived at and as reflected in *price,* is the basis for determining value in accounting. It is supportable by objective, verifiable evidence. Liabilities and proprietorship claims are also encompassed in the framework of *value in exchange* because they, too, involve market transactions and frequently originate concurrently with the exchange of goods or services.

2. *Cost.* The price set in an exchange in which goods or services are acquired is referred to as *cost.* This is value in exchange as applied to acquisitions. Assets are valued at such cost which is also referred to as *acquisition cost.* Once assets have been so stated they are accounted for on that basis and the values do not change or fluctuate except to the extent that they have lost the utility to the company which they had at the time of acquisition. Such diminution in utility occurs as assets are used up and are reflected in depreciation or amortization entries or in transfers to other expense or even, sometimes, to loss accounts.

3. *Historical cost.* Accounting is often referred to as dealing with *historical cost,* that is, with original cost as further adjusted by depreciation and similar entries based on such cost. This basis, which conforms with generally accepted accounting principles, is so referred to when it is desired to contrast it with proposed systems of accounting based on current values or replacement costs.

Certain assets like accounts or notes receivable are not usually purchased but originate from revenue transactions. It is awkward to apply the term *cost* to such assets, but they do originate from the same type of economic exchange. The expression "assets are stated at cost" also covers such assets.

4. *Market value.* This term has various applications in accounting. In general, it connotes the price which would have to be paid for goods or services if acquired at some specified time, or would be received if sold. If assets are received in exchange for capital stock or other assets, they must be stated at cost but, in the absence of bargained price, the market value at date of acquisition would be taken as the equivalent of "cash cost." Inventories are frequently stated at "the lower of cost or market," in which case market might be determined by reference to *replacement market* or *selling market* (that is, expected sales price or realizable value). When marketable securities are stated at the lower of cost or market, the latter connotes the expected selling price. Since assets are accounted for on a cost basis, market enters into the accounting for certain assets only when in the appropriate situation the applicable "market" provides a measure of the decline in the utility attached to original cost. Only under unusual circumstances (for example, quasi-reorganization) are asset values adjusted upward to market values.

5. *Liquidation value.* This is a form of market value and represents the expected proceeds from the sale of assets upon a forced sale or a liquidation of individual assets or the entire business.

6. *Replacement value or reproduction cost.* Replacement value (one type of market value) is the estimated cost of currently replacing an asset. It is called *reproduction cost* when applied to manufactured goods.

7. *Present value.* This concept of value recognizes that money or other assets have different values at different points in time. The *present value* of an asset is the expected future value discounted to the current date at some appropriate discount rate. For example, an account receivable of $10,000 due in one year may be said to have a *current value* of $9,425 if the discount rate is 6% and is compounded semiannually. Under the present value concept, the creditor would be in the same position if he were currently to settle the account for $9,425 as he would be if the loan were allowed to run for the full year, because the sum of $9,425 if invested at 6% would accumulate to $10,000 one year hence. This concept is viewed by many economists as a desirable basis for current valuation of assets and of the entity as a whole. Such current values would be the *present value* of all future financial benefits derivable from the assets. The term *service potential* is sometimes used to describe these future benefits. This method, however, can be characterized as an abstraction which is impracticable. Only in rare circumstances is this method of recording assets acceptable to accounting. It is too

highly fraught with conjecture and possibly simple guesswork, involving as it does predictions as to the course of future events.

VALUE IN EXCHANGE

To be acceptable to accounting, values must be objectively arrived at and supported by verifiable evidence. Values in exchange as evidenced in completed market transactions meet these standards. Assets acquired for use by the accounting entity are stated at their value in exchange—that is, at their cost price. Assets which originate in revenue transactions, like accounts receivable or notes receivable, similarly enter into the accounts at their values in exchange—in this instance, equal to the sales price. Liabilities which arise when assets are purchased or expenses are incurred are also expressed on the same basis—that is, at values derived from such exchanges. Liabilities which arise in loan transactions, like notes payable to banks or bonds payable, are similarly measured in amounts determined in the "market." All these prices and values, based as they are on consummated events in an objective market place, are definite, objective, and verifiable.

Even a market exchange may give rise to misleading values if it is a sham or is otherwise unreliable and does not occur in a true market. An objective market will yield objective values whose economic significance for the particular entity corresponds to their significance generally for any other entity similarly situated. It is, therefore, to be understood that an objective market implies the following characteristics.

1. *Arms-length.* The transaction must be on an arms-length basis and devoid of collusive arrangements.

2. *Bargained price.* The reality and objectivity of value in exchange are confirmed to the extent that the parties sincerely engaged in the act of bargaining which is a conventional feature of market dealings.

3. *Rationality.* The more rational the conduct of the participating parties, the more it is assured that the exchange values decided upon would have comparable economic significance for any prudent individual.

4. *Representativeness of market prices.* An objective market implies that there is sufficient activity in the market to permit the emergence of prices which are truly indicative of market values.

5. *Individuality of market.* Various markets may be pertinent to the entity depending on the character of the entity and the goods or services exchanged. The appropriate market may be retail or wholesale; market prices may vary with quantities, type of goods or services, or location. Market values are judged in accounting by reference to the market most appropriate for the entity under the given surrounding circumstances.

6. *Legality.* It is assumed that market transactions have their confirmation in law and are evidenced by documents and other matter which have legal import.

The concept of value in exchange may be succinctly stated in the following terms:

Upon their initial emergence in the accounting process, the resources (assets) of an entity and any corresponding claims against them (liabilities and equities) are assigned values based upon the prices and money amounts as stated in consummated exchange transactions occurring in an objective market.

This concept underlies such principles as "assets are recorded at cost" or "income is not recognized unless actually realized" (that is, as evidenced by completed transactions such as a sale). But the reader may find it difficult to reconcile the proposition with the recording of inventories or marketable securities at market where market is less than cost. It should be remembered, however, that the concept refers to values originating in consummated transactions only for the initial recording of data. Any write-down of inventories or securities to market is based, to be sure, on an *expected* market value and not on a completed transaction, but such a write-down is not a recording of the *initial emergence* of the asset.

UTILITY AND ASSET VALUES

Goods or services are acquired because of the utility which they have for the purchaser. Value in exchange provides an objective measure of the utility of these resources as of the date of acquisition. If the exchange transactions have occurred in an objective market, there is a strong presumption that the utility of the resources to the entity at that date corresponds to their true economic utility or value.

But what happens to these values and to the utility which they reflect subsequent to their emergence in the accounts? How accounting views the initial values and how it accounts for later changes may be explained in the following terms.

1. *Effort and accomplishment.* Resources have value because of the contribution or effort which they are capable of making toward the accomplishment of the entity's objectives. The reader may wish to refer, in this connection, to the earlier discussion on the form and content of financial statements.

2. *Value and utility.* The value of an asset is dependent on its economic utility.

3. *Varying types of utility.* Each asset exhibits a type of utility peculiar to that asset. Fixed assets, for example, have their utility in their productive use and not in cash realizability upon sale. Inventories are held with a view to selling them at a profit, whereas accounts receivable have a utility to the extent that they can be collected and the cash equivalent realized. Cash itself has intrinsic and unchanging utility (except, of course, for price-level changes) because of its universal exchange value.

4. *Historical record.* Accounting views the initially recorded values of assets in relationship to the purpose for which these assets are held. Accounting therefore provides an historical record of what happens to these assets and their initial values from the time of acquisition to the time their purpose is fulfilled.

5. *Retention of value.* An asset retains its value in the absence of evidence that it will fail to yield the expected results.

6. *Transferability of value.* When a variety of assets enter into the achievement of a single result and there are various stages in the efforts expended to achieve that result, asset values are transferable from stage to stage. Thus direct labor costs become part of inventory costs. Depreciation represents a transfer of fixed asset values to inventories. Values, however, are still retained in such transfers.

7. *Decline in value.* A decline in the value of an asset as originally recorded takes place when there is reasonable evidence that such value is no longer a measure of the asset's remaining utility. As an example, depreciation or amortization of fixed or intangible assets represents a reduction in asset values corresponding to the reduction in remaining useful life. A write-down of the inventories from cost to, say, replacement market is made on the theory that the lower replacement market will result in lower selling prices, and original cost is therefore no longer a proper measure of the utility of the inventories.

An allowance for bad debts is recorded in the expectation that the full amount of the receivables may not be collected.

It should be noted that the term *reasonable evidence* rather than *objective, verifiable evidence* has been used for gauging the decline in values. The reason is that we are dealing with expectations rather than with consummated transactions. The concept of objectivity ensures that such reasonable evidence will be as objective as the circumstances allow.

8. *Expiration of value.* Assets are partially or completely eliminated from the accounts to the extent that they have been utilized for their intended purpose in order to properly match cost and revenue. Thus inventories are transferred to cost of sales when a sale has been made. Through periodic depreciation, fixed assets become fully depreciated at the expiration of their useful lives. Marketable securities are eliminated when sold by transfer to a gain or loss account. Accounts receivable are credited as cash is received from customers.

9. *Changes in use of assets.* A basic change in the original use of an asset calls for a modification in the criteria for judging its utility. If fixed assets, for example, are removed from productive use and held for sale, then the remaining balance of the originally recorded cost must be evaluated in terms of the expected results of the new use to which it has been put—the anticipated sales price of the assets. If the latter is below cost, a write-down would be indicated.

10. *Increases in value.* Accounting does not recognize increases in values for retained assets. Assets may be exchanged for other assets having an exchange value higher than the asset given up and the acquired asset will be stated at the exchange value. But the assets formerly held are accounted for, up to the date of exchange, on the basis of original cost less any recorded declines in value.

11. *Utility to the individual entity.* Accounting judges the continued utility of an asset by reference to its utility for the specific entity. Such assets as cash, accounts receivable, and marketable securities have a utility which is common to all entities. But the utility of assets like inventories, fixed assets, or intangibles will depend on the individual circumstances surrounding the particular entity. One enterprise may follow a policy of replacing machinery every five years, whereas another company may have different standards for obsolescence and may depreciate similar machinery over a ten-year period. There are times when an enterprise may be able to sell its inventories only at a loss, whereas other enterprises are able to sell comparable

merchandise at a normal profit. Since accounting describes the activities of a particular entity, it is the utility of assets to the particular entity that counts. To be sure, the ultimate results from the use of assets will be determined in the external economic environment where exchanges take place, but anticipated results, as we have indicated, do enter into the measurement of declines in asset values.

The concept of utility and asset values may be expressed in the following terms:

Assets are accounted for on the basis of their originally recorded values; a reduction in the value of an asset is recorded when there is reasonable evidence that such value ceases to be a proper measure of the asset's remaining utility to the entity.

ACCOUNTING PERIOD

If economic entities which form the subject matter of accounting existed simply to carry on a single short-term venture and were to pass out of existence upon the completion of the venture, the body of accounting knowledge would become greatly simplified. The net results of the entity's activities would be readily established by subtracting the values contributed to the venture from the values remaining upon liquidation. The determination of earnings would be definitive if cash were contributed and the resources remaining at the end also consisted exclusively of cash. If there were a need for financial statements prior to completion of the venture, the statements would be a relatively simple affair showing the resources contributed to the venture and the claims against them. Because of the short-term character of the venture, the need would not usually arise for an interim determination of income.

The life of an entity is currently regarded as consisting of a chain of one-year segments. Interim financial statements are frequently prepared on a monthly, quarterly, or semiannual basis, but the statements which report on the activities for a year and the condition of the entity as of the close of that year are regarded as the *final* statements. Many writers refer to this practice as the *accounting period convention.*

Enterprises retain their identity for long periods of time and their activities consist of continuous streams of economic undertakings, many of which are involved and intertwined and bear little resemblance to clear-cut identifiable short-term ventures. The practical demands of society for periodic reporting make it impossible to postpone the communication of the results of an entity's activities to the time of its liquidation. Investors, creditors, and the entity itself require timely periodic reports as a basis for informed judgments and decisions. The fact that reports cover periods of equal length is of great importance in facilitating comparisons of operating results from period to period and in analyzing long-term trends.

It is the accounting period concept which gives rise to the complex problems of accounting—the determination of net income, the valuation of assets to be carried forward to the subsequent period, and the entire system of accruals, deferrals, and allocation of income, expense, and costs. While the preparation of annual reports is simply a fact—a convention dictated by the economic and business environment—accounting theory is affected by that fact. Many of the undertakings of an entity are uncompleted at any given point in time. The final results will be known only when the enterprise is liquidated Reports for a short-run period must, therefore, be tentative. Hence, a concept is required which says, in effect, that the fairness of presentation of the results of an entity's operations is not affected by the fact that the report covers only a specified period rather than an entire life span.

Moreover, since the accounting period is the focal unit for the assignment of values which enter into the efforts, accomplishments, and net results for that period, we must also postulate that values are indeed capable of being allocated to accounting periods. A proposition on the allocability of values is needed as a basis for amortization of fixed or intangible assets over time periods, for the accrual of items such as interest income or expense which grow with the passage of time, for the deferral to a succeeding accounting period of income or costs such as unearned income or prepaid expenses, and the like. The following proposition has been framed with these considerations in mind:

The results of an entity's operations are reportable in sequential periods of time, and accounting values have the attribute of being allocable, when necessary, to accounting periods.

THE ENTITY AS A GOING CONCERN

The accounting period concept is closely related to the concept which views the entity as a going concern. The latter is sometimes referred to as the continuity concept. It states, in effect, the following:

Unless and until the entity has entered into a state of liquidation, it is to be viewed as having an indefinite life.

The following are some of the significant ideas which underlie the going concern concept.

1. *Closing values.* The activities of an entity consist of continuous streams of undertakings which may be in various stages of completion at the close of any given accounting period. The values which remain at the close of a period are carried forward to the next.

2. *Consequences.* Here are some of the consequences of the going concern convention in the valuation of certain accounts, in contrast to those which would prevail if accounting had adopted, instead, a liquidation concept:

(a) *Investments.* These assets, if current, are recorded at the lower of cost or market or, if noncurrent, at cost, unless there has been a permanent and substantial decline in market value. A liquidation approach would require an adjustment to market.

(b) Inventories. Assuming the continuity of the entity, inventories are stated at the lower of cost or market but, in the event of liquidation, values would be stated at realizable value which, on a forced sale, could be substantially below normal selling prices and even below replacement market.

(c) *Long-term assets.* In the absence of a continuity convention, some intangibles would have to be completely written off as valueless. Fixed assets, whose utility is judged in terms of their continued productive use, would be valued in terms of the amounts which could be realized in a second-hand market.

(d) *Prepaid insurance.* In the event of liquidation, the usual computation of prepaid insurance based on a straight pro-rata apportionment of the premium would give way to a short-term cancellation calculation of the unexpired premium.

3. *The idea of indefinite life.* Accounting does not arbitrarily assume that an entity has an indefinite life. It recognizes that there are many entities which do endure for long periods of time while others may last for just a short period and, in fact, may go into bankruptcy shortly after their inception. But accounting does not engage in supposition and conjecture as to whether this or that entity has reached the point where the possibility of liquidation must be contemplated, or when the liquidation is likely to take place. The

system of accounting theory is designed to portray the financial condition of an enterprise. If there has been a history of losses or the financial condition of a company otherwise reflects instability, these data will be reflected in the financial statements and appropriate inferences and conclusions can be drawn by the reader of the financial statements.

4. *Formal liquidation.* Accounting does not explicitly recognize or disclose a liquidation condition, even if imminent, unless and until the entity by expressed intention or action, has formalized the plan to liquidate. A number of writers express the going-concern idea somewhat as follows: "In the absence of evidence to the contrary, the entity is to be viewed as having an indefinite life." This statement, however, does not, in our opinion, correctly reflect generally accepted accounting theory on this point. Even if there were evidence that the entity may have a limited life, this fact would not by itself affect the going-concern approach in the absence of an intention to liquidate or a course of action that would so indicate. Evidence of a limited life simply constitutes essential knowledge to be used in valuing specific assets and in estimating, for example, the remaining period of useful life of amortizable assets.

5. *Company size and stability.* Accounting theory does not explicitly provide for distinctions such as the following which may have bearing on the going-concern character of an enterprise: large or small concerns; long or short period of prior existence; history of losses or earnings; extent of stability or fluctuation in past operating results; conventionality or speculativeness of business operations. However, accounting judgment takes into consideration the individual circumstances of a company in the selection of appropriate accounting methods. Moreover, the past performance of a company and its current condition and prospects are factors which enter into judgment as to the period of amortization of intangibles or fixed assets or the accrual of estimated liabilities. Thus, for example, if a company has been operating at a loss and its character as a going concern is seriously in question, a judgment may be made that certain long-term assets should be amortized over a shorter remaining life than hitherto estimated.

MEANING OF CONSERVATISM

The concept of *conservatism* is so thoroughly identified with accounting practice and plays such a significant role in effectuating certain accounting results that it must be regarded as a major element in the structure of accounting theory. The concept may be expressed as follows:

Conservatism is a necessary condition for the fair presentation of accounting data.

Conservatism comes into play when events or activities which must be reflected in the accounting process are characterized by uncertainty about their outcome and an accounting judgment must be made in selecting an appropriate accounting method or procedure from among various alternatives. As used in accounting, the term *conservatism* connotes moderation, caution, and avoidance of unnecessary risk in terms of the accounting results. As between a showing of greater or lesser accomplishments, accounting interprets a possible overstatement of net income, assets, and net worth or understatement of liabilities as being more hazardous and, therefore, less conservative than a possible understatement of net income, assets, and net worth or overstatement of liabilities. (In the event of uncertainty, therefore, conservatism will help to resolve any reasonable doubts in the formulation of accounting decisions in favor of that procedure which achieves conservative results.)

Question—May 1951 (5)

Accountants frequently refer to a procedure as being conservative. Explain what is meant by "conservative accounting" procedures. Discuss the question of the extent to which it is possible to follow accounting procedures which will result in consistently conservative financial statements over a considerable number of years.

Solution

1. *Relativity of concept.* Conservatism is a relative concept. An accounting procedure may be said to be more or less conservative than one or more other procedures which could have been used.

2. *Effect on balance sheet.* As applied to the balance sheet, a conservative procedure is one which produces a lower valuation of assets and capital, or a greater amount of liabilities, than another procedure which might alternatively have been used.

3. *Effect on income.* A conservative procedure is one which results in a lower net income than would otherwise be the case.

4. *Uncertainty.* Conservatism acts as a guide where there are un-

certainties inherent in the activity, transaction, or event which is the subject matter to be recorded in the accounts.

5. *Examples of uncertainty.* There may be uncertainty as to the: (a) useful life of amortizable assets such as fixed assets or intangibles; (b) occurrence of a loss; (c) realization of income; (d) remaining utility of an asset; (e) estimated liabilities or valuation accounts.

6. *Equally acceptable methods.* In the event of uncertainty, conservatism dictates the choice of that method, from among one or more other generally accepted methods, which will achieve conservative results for the balance sheet and the income statement.

7. *Estimates.* When amounts are based on estimates and a reasonable doubt exists as to which one of several amounts is the most accurate, conservatism would select that amount which yields the lower asset valuation, lower net income, etc.

8. *Useful life.* There may be doubt as to whether the useful life of fixed or intangible assets is, say, five, six, or seven years. The choice of a five-year life is more conservative than six, and six more conservative than seven because of the lower asset value and lower earnings which result from the faster write-off.

9. *Accounting method.* Another illustration of conservatism is evidenced by the difference between declining-balance depreciation and straight-line depreciation. If a period of useful life has been decided upon but there remain doubts as to the period of useful life or the extent of utilization of assets in the later years, then conservatism might lead to the choice of declining-balance depreciation which results in a faster write-off in the earlier years. But it is important to stress the point that conservatism does not necessarily mean that an accounting method is selected simply because it will result in the *lowest* valuation of assets and the *lowest* earnings.

10. *Losses and profits.* Accounting recognizes losses before they actually occur if they originate in conditions existing at or prior to the balance sheet date, but it does not record profits until they are realized. These principles are based, in part, on the concept of conservatism.

11. *Short-run effect.* Over a short period of several years, a consistent policy of conservatism will usually result in a continued understatement of net assets and earnings. Thus, for example, if fixed assets are being depreciated over a five-year period instead of, alternatively, a longer period, the financial statements will show the conservative effects over the five-year period. If major repairs are expensed in circumstances where doubt existed as to the propriety of

capitalization as fixed assets, the balance sheet and income statement for that year will reflect conservative results.

12. *Long-run effect.* Over the long run, however, a conservative procedure achieves unconservative results. Thus if it develops, for example, that fixed assets have a longer life than originally anticipated, then the net income for the later years will be higher than they would have been if the longer period had been originally selected as the basis for depreciation. Over the long run, conservatism does not achieve consistent results. The balance sheet, it is true, continues to be conservative, but less and less so as time goes on. The income statement, however, at a certain point becomes nonconservative and reflects higher profits than would otherwise be the case.

13. *Conservatism and misrepresentation.* It would be incorrect to identify conservatism with misrepresentation of financial condition or operating results or with deliberate understatement of assets, net worth, and earnings, unless the conservative procedure was also an unacceptable one in the circumstances. It is the factor of uncertainty, in the first instance, which requires that a choice be made from among reasonable alternatives. Conservatism does not lessen uncertainty; it seeks merely to minimize the hazards which can result when accounting judgments are required to be made despite doubts as to how future events may actually turn out. The theory is that, if there is a choice between *possible* understatement of assets and income and possible overstatement, the readers of financial statements are less likely to be misled if the method selected achieves the former result.

14. *Understatement and overstatement.* Consider the assertion that conservatism understates assets and income in earlier years and overstates income in later years thereby resulting in periodic income statements which are not comparable. Such an assertion can only be made "after the fact" and on the basis of hindsight after future events have unfolded. Future events may confirm the reliability of the "conservative" estimate or they may reveal that the original estimate should have been more or less conservative. If it is conceded that accounting must deal with uncertainties, then the possibility of understatement or overstatement must be acknowledged to be inherent in the accounting process. This would be so regardless of whether the concept employed entails conservatism or nonconservatism. It is, therefore, improper to use the terms *understatement* or *overstatement* in this connection to connote willful misstatement of the accounts. But an accounting method which violates generally accepted

accounting principles remains unacceptable regardless of its conservatism.

15. *Fairness of presentation.* Conservatism is only one element entering into an accounting judgment which, in any given situation, would weigh the factor of conservatism in a delicate balance along with other factors in an effort to arrive at an informed judgment as to the fairest estimate.

APPLICATIONS OF CONSERVATISM

Conservatism can find expression in almost any area of accounting. It will be helpful, however, to attempt a classification of those occasions with which it is most often identified.

1. *Useful life of amortizable assets.* Conservatism provides a guide to judgment when there is uncertainty as to the period over which fixed, intangible, and other long-term assets are to be amortized.

2. *Indefinite life.* Certain intangibles or other assets may have an indefinite life and might not normally be subject to amortization. In individual circumstances, however, conservatism will tend to encourage the adoption of a systematic plan of amortization over some reasonable period.

3. *Accelerated depreciation.* Although a reasonable estimate may be made of the period of useful life of fixed assets, that method may be selected which results in higher depreciation charges in the earlier years. In this sense, declining-balance depreciation or the sum-of-the-years-digits method may be said to be more conservative than, say, the straight-line or units-of-production methods.

4. *Income and losses.* The principle that income should not be recognized until actually realized, while losses should be anticipated, is often cited as an illustration of conservatism. Inventories, for example, are written down to market, if lower than cost, but never raised to market, if higher than cost. Conservatism, however, is only one of the elements which enters into this principle. The nonrecognition of income is primarily based upon the concept that assets do not emerge except through consummated exchange transactions occurring in an objective market, and upon the concept of utility and asset values according to which assets are accounted for on the basis of their originally recorded values except for the recognition of decline in value.

5. *Liabilities versus surplus reserve.* A decision as to whether an item is to be reflected as an estimated liability or simply disclosed in the form of a footnote or surplus reserve, frequently revolves around the extent of uncertainty of the occurrence of an event, say, an unfavorable judgment in a pending law suit. Depending upon the degree of uncertainty, conservatism would swing the decision in the direction of recording the probable loss and the corresponding liability.

6. *Capital versus revenue.* It is sometimes difficult to decide whether an item should be capitalized as an asset or charged off to revenues. A common illustration of this would be a major repair of fixed assets. There may be conflicting beliefs as to whether the efficiency or useful life of the machine, for example, has been sufficiently enhanced or extended to warrant capitalizing the cost of the major repairs. It would be more "conservative," of course, to expense the cost.

7. *Estimated amounts.* Even the amount at which an account is stated may be influenced by conservatism. Assuming that conservatism has chosen between an estimated liability and a surplus reserve, it continues to exert its influence relative to the amount at which the estimated liability is recorded, say, for estimated warranty costs, taxes, and lawsuit damages. Doubt as to which of several amounts would be reasonable would be resolved in favor of the higher amounts. The same would be true for an account like the allowance for bad debts. But in the event of uncertainty as to the amount of accrued income, conservatism would stress the lower estimate.

8. *Current versus noncurrent.* In some situations the classification of an asset or liability in the current or noncurrent sections of the balance sheet may pose a problem. A receivable, for example, may be fully collectible but has been past due for a considerable period. A long-term debt may fall due in the following year and there may be doubts as to whether it can be refunded. Bearing in mind the relevance of the concept of uncertainty, it is more conservative to show an asset as noncurrent rather than current and a liability as current rather than noncurrent.

9. *Inception of business.* In the early period of an entity's life, losses may be incurred in the process of getting started. Sometimes, certain expenses, including preoperating expenses, which entered into the net loss may actually have a value for future operations and should therefore be shown as prepaid expenses or deferred charges to expense. Where the future utility of the items is in question, however, the conservative procedure would call for expensing them. An attitude of conservatism is especially held by accountants in the early stages of a company's life because the company has not as yet established

itself as a going concern, and its future, in general, may be quite uncertain.

10. *History of losses.* Accountants tend to apply the doctrine of conservatism more sharply when a company has had a long history of losses or if its financial condition for other reasons is precarious. Because of the possibility of future insolvency, the accountant is apt to be especially alert to the hazards which this condition might have for creditors and credit grantors. He would also be keenly sensitive to potential criticism by them and possibly by dissenting stockholder interests that the assets and income have been overstated and that a less favorable presentation would have put them on timely notice so that their interests could have been protected sooner.

SIGNIFICANCE OF CONSERVATISM FOR VARIOUS PARTIES

Conservatism in accounting originally reflected the concern of the credit grantor that asset values might be overstated or liabilities understated, with the result that the financial position of the debtor or potential borrower might be portrayed in an unduly favorable light. When the emphasis changed from the balance sheet to the income statement, conservatism was considered to apply equally to the determination of income. The following discussion considers the effect of conservatism on each of the important segments of society who may rely on the financial reports.

1. *Credit grantors.* The amount of a loan extended by a credit grantor will obviously be based on the company's financial position and history of earnings, but for many companies the emphasis is on the balance sheet and the capacity of the debtor to liquidate the loan. If the financial position is at least as favorable as it is represented to be, the credit grantor has that additional protection which acts as a "cushion" in the event of future unfavorable results. Moreover, the size of the loan is probably smaller than it would have been otherwise. In addition, the "less favorable" results achieved by conservatism would cause the credit grantor to initiate personal inquiries in order to acquaint himself more directly with the company's condition and operations.

2. *The entity.* In the absence of conservatism, the entity itself may engage in certain actions to its detriment. It may so obligate itself financially that, if its optimistic expectations do not materialize, it may find itself in difficult financial straits. Thus dividends may be disbursed, replacement programs undertaken, and liabilities incurred beyond what would have been the case if conservative accounting procedures had been adopted.

3. *Potential investors.* Those who plan to purchase stock in a company have the same measure of protection as the credit grantor. Conservatism provides the assurance that the financial position and earnings of a company are at least as favorable as they are represented to be.

4. *Seller of stock interest.* Although it is true that conservatism appears to operate to the detriment of the seller of securities, an informed investor would be expected to understand the assumptions and principles which underlie the financial statements and to take these into consideration.

5. *Buyer or seller of business.* Although the financial statements provide a guide to the sales price of a business or of specific assets, it is customary for statement figures to be adjusted in the course of negotiations. It is generally recognized that the financial statements reflect going-concern values and that these values, however conservatively they may have been stated, will be adjusted in special reports prepared for the benefit of the negotiating parties.

CONSISTENCY

Accounting theory and the accounting mechanism have as their objective the fair portrayal of an entity's condition and operations. Realities lie outside the accounting framework and it is the task of the latter to describe these realities. It is possible, however, for the accounting structure itself to be the instrumentality for creating an impression that external changes or events have taken place when, in fact, such has not been the case. An important example of this is a change in accounting method—that is, an inconsistency in the application of accounting principles. Formally expressed, this concept would read:

Financial statements are prepared on a basis consistent with that of the preceding periods; if changes are made in the application of accounting principles or methods, the effects of such changes on the accounting presentation are disclosed.

Question—November 1958 (3a)

What does the term *consistency* mean as it is used in accounting?

Solution

1. *Accounting principles and their application.* The idea of consistency embraces not only accounting principles but also the accounting practices and methods of applying these principles.

2. *Alternative accounting methods.* There are many areas of accounting in which alternative accounting methods may be used in applying accounting principles, and such methods may be equally acceptable. For example, in applying the principle that fixed assets are depreciated over the period of useful life, a company may choose from among the following depreciation methods: straight-line, declining-balance, sum-of-the years-digits, units-of-production, etc.

3. *Consistency and inconsistency.* Consistency refers to the use of the same accounting principles or methods from year to year. It is always understood that consistency will be observed within each period. An inconsistency in the application of accounting principles would result if the method were changed in one year as compared with the preceding year, even if there were sound reasons for the change.

4. *Comparability.* Long-term trends and comparison of financial data from year to year are extremely useful in analyzing the affairs of a company. Such comparisons are no less important than an evaluation of the financial statements for a single year. Consistency, therefore, contributes to the comparability of the current year's financial statements with those of prior periods.

5. *Effect on balance sheet and income.* A change in accounting principles or methods, even without any actual change in business operations, can result in a higher or lower asset valuation or a higher or lower reported income than would otherwise be the case. An emphasis on consistency therefore precludes any attempt to arbitrarily affect the financial condition of a company or to capriciously or deliberately shift income from one accounting period to another.

6. *Misleading inferences.* In the absence of this doctrine of consistency, misleading inferences might be drawn by the readers of the financial statements who may attribute the changes in operating results or in balance sheet data to actual happenings.

7. *Permissible changes.* Accounting methods may be changed when there is a sound reason for the change; usually, however, the reason need be no stronger than the general belief, for which no special support is normally required, that the new method is equally (or more) appropriate in the circumstances. To be sure, the new method must be generally accepted; it is also assumed that such changes

are infrequent and are not part of an ulterior design to manipulate or otherwise misrepresent the financial data.

8. *Unacceptable method.* As mentioned previously, the change must be to a generally accepted accounting method. If the new method is unacceptable, there would be not only an inconsistency but also a violation of accounting principles.

9. *Disclosure.* It is management's responsibility to disclose the nature of the change and its effect on both balance sheet and income statement. The disclosure is made in a note to the financial statements and thereby provides the information needed to judge adequately the effect of the inconsistency on the comparability of the current year's statement with those of prior years.

CONSISTENCY AND CONSERVATISM

Some writers contend that conservatism and consistency are incompatible and that conservatism must give rise to inconsistencies. Several examples will help to clarify the basis on which this argument rests and to point up the misunderstanding which sometimes develops when the term consistency is not used in its technical accounting sense.

Question—November 1958 (3c)

Give one illustration of the application of a rule of conservatism which results in an apparent inconsistency. Explain.

Solution

Any one of the following will serve as an illustration of apparent inconsistency.

1. *Shift in income.* If conservatism leads to the selection of a shorter period of usefulness of depreciable property, to the choice of an accelerated method of depreciation, or to the expensing of an asset in a "capital versus revenue" situation, an understatement of income in the current year or in several succeeding years will result in an overstatement of income in later years. It is incorrect to refer to this as an *inconsistency*, because no change in accounting method is involved. The same accounting methods may have been consistently used. The conservative procedure may have an effect on the

comparability of income over the years. Conservatism is an essential guide in conditions of uncertainty and should not be identified either with inconsistency or shifting of income unless the concept of conservatism is misapplied.

2. *Basis of valuation.* The principle of "lower of cost or market" as a basis for inventory valuation seems to point to an inconsistency if cost is used one year and, when cost is higher than market, market is used in another year. Since this practice reflects the proper use of the single accounting method of "lower of cost or market," there has been no change in method and no inconsistency. The shift in reference point from cost to market was simply an application of the one method.

3. *Losses and revenue.* If circumstances indicate that losses or declines in asset values have occurred, they are recorded even if the events which conclusively establish these losses have not yet materialized. On the other hand, revenue is not recorded until actually realized. Inventories or marketable securities will be valued at market if this is lower than cost, and the loss will thus be recognized prior to sale, but gains will not be recorded until the assets are sold. Estimated future expenses applicable to the current period are recorded, but anticipated profits are not. These variations may be termed an *inconsistency,* but it is not so in the technical sense of a change in method. The rule that losses, but not profits, are anticipated merely means that there are certain principles that govern the treatment of losses and different principles that apply to the realization of income. This difference is mistakenly referred to as an inconsistency.

The subject of consistency and comparability is developed further in Chapter 4, particularly with respect to the technical reporting rules for both management and the independent auditor.

MISUSE OF ACCOUNTING MECHANISM

In introducing the subject of consistency, we said that the accounting mechanism itself may be misused for the purpose of achieving an unfair presentation. Because the accounting framework is the medium by which realities are portrayed, an accounting presentation is looked upon by the reader as a representation of those realities. Any improper presentation such as the following will therefore misrepresent the actual happenings.

1. *Expenses charged to balance sheet credit accounts.* Certain credit accounts like capital surplus, surplus reserves, and unrealized income have been used to overstate income by the technique of charging those accounts with expenses or losses which should have been charged to income.

2. *Offsets of assets against liabilities.* When there are credit balances in the accounts receivable account or debit balances in the accounts payable account, a company may find it to its advantage to avoid adjusting the accounts so that assets and liabilities may be separately and clearly disclosed. There is a general rule in accounting which forbids the offset of assets against liabilities.

FULL DISCLOSURE

In the absence of an accounting concept requiring appropriate disclosure of material matters, the formal compliance with the generally accepted concepts and principles of accounting may not necessarily result in financial statements which are fair presentations. It is possible to have simply technical or token adherence to accounting requirements and yet fail to achieve the degree of informative disclosure of significant data necessary to make the financial statements not misleading. The idea of full disclosure may be expressed somewhat as follows:

A fair accounting presentation necessitates the full disclosure of material information.

The extent and nature of informative disclosures are necessarily dependent upon the exercise of judgment in the individual circumstances of a particular entity. Certain general rules, however, have been set forth in authoritative accounting literature which suggest the general areas and types of disclosure. These rules, as well as the independent auditor's responsibilities in complying with the standard of reporting dealing with informative disclosures, are discussed in Chapter 4.

In general, it is expected that any matter of significance such as major contingencies or commitments will be disclosed if knowledge of it would affect the decision of an average prudent reader of the financial statements. The term *full disclosure* does not mean that any and all information that anyone could conceivably desire is to be included in the accounting statements or in appended notes. The term implies that there is to be adequate disclosure of information which is of material interest to those segments of society—the credit grantor, the stockholder, potential investor, and the entity itself—who make use of general-purpose financial statements and reports.

MATERIALITY

The concept of materiality plays a major part in the application of accounting principles and in the standards of reporting. It is obvious that accounting would assume an unnecessary and impossible burden if it failed to distinguish between material and immaterial matters. This distinction is implied in the introduction to ARB No. 43:

> "The Committee contemplates that its opinions will have application only to items material and significant in the relative circumstances. It considers that items of little or no consequence may be dealt with as expediency may suggest. However, freedom to deal expediently with immaterial items should not extend to a group of items whose cumulative effect in any one financial statement may be material and significant."

The term *materiality* is used in many of the AICPA's pronouncements but is not defined. The SEC defines materiality in Rule 1-02 of *Regulation S-X* as follows:

> "The term 'material,' when used to qualify a requirement for the furnishing of information as to any subject, limits the information required to those matters as to which an average prudent investor ought reasonably to be informed before purchasing the security registered."

The definition advanced by the AAA (1957 Revision) explains the term in a similar vein, substituting the adjective *informed* for *average prudent* in referring to the investor:

> "An item should be regarded as material if there is reason to believe that knowledge of it would influence the decisions of an informed investor."

Despite the importance of the concept of materiality, only the SEC has provided specific criteria for judging materiality, and then only selectively in certain disclosure situations referred to in *Regulation*

S-X. The general understanding is that what is material can be gauged only by individual judgment. Consequently, in the absence of specific criteria, the concept of materiality makes its impact on the accountant in a general and diffuse way. It serves to instill a sense of alertness and vigilance, and a sensitivity to the necessary requirements if the financial statements are not to be misleading. In the final analysis, the proof of the proper exercise of accounting judgment as to what is material can be established only when, in an individual case, the charge is made that the concept of materiality has been disregarded and a successful defense is made against that charge.

AUDITING AND ACCOUNTING THEORY

The verification principles, procedures, and standards followed by the independent auditor in undertaking his examination and in rendering his report constitute the separate subject of auditing. Auditing, however, is closely related to accounting theory inasmuch as the auditor is required to express in his report an unqualified opinion, a qualified opinion, or an adverse opinion (or, under certain circumstances, disclaim an opinion) with respect to whether the financial position of the company and the results of operations are fairly presented in conformity with generally accepted accounting principles applied on a basis consistent with the preceding reporting period. To form a proper opinion, the auditor must comply with auditing standards and undertake auditing procedures which enable him to *verify* whether, in fact, management has prepared the statements in conformity with accepted accounting principles on a consistent basis.

Of the ten auditing standards, the four standards of reporting are of immediate interest. These require that the auditor express in his report the following:

1. Whether the statements are in conformity with generally accepted accounting principles.

2. Whether these principles have been consistently observed.

3. Informative disclosures on material matters which were not disclosed by management either in the financial statements or in the appended notes.

4. Either an opinion—unqualified, qualified or adverse—or a disclaimer together with the reasons for the disclaimer.

The following opinion paragraph of the standard short-form audit report illustrates how the auditor complies with these standards when issuing an unqualified opinion.

Opinion paragraph—unqualified opinion

In our opinion, the accompanying balance sheet and statements of income and retained earnings present fairly the financial position of the Client Corporation at June 30, 1967, and the results of its operations for the year then ended, in conformity with generally accepted accounting principles applied on a basis consistent with that of the preceding year.

In general, the difference between a qualified opinion and an adverse opinion is one of degree in the materiality and significance of the qualifications rather than of type of circumstance. In an adverse opinion the auditor states that the financial statements do not present fairly the financial position or results of operations in conformity with generally accepted accounting principles. Statement on Auditing Procedure No. 33 offers the following as an illustration of an adverse opinion.

Opinion paragraph—adverse opinion expressed

Because of the materiality of the amounts of omitted income taxes as described in the preceding paragraph, we are of the opinion that the financial statements do not present fairly the financial position of the Client Corporation at June 30, 1967 or the results of its operations for the year then ended in conformity with generally accepted accounting principles.

GENERALLY ACCEPTED ACCOUNTING PRINCIPLES AND THE AUDITOR'S STANDARD OF REPORTING NO. 1

The first reporting standard is as follows:

The report shall state whether the financial statements are presented in accordance with generally accepted principles of accounting.

The standard imposes on the independent accountant the obligation to state in his report whether the financial statements are presented in accordance with generally accepted principles of accounting. The auditor complies with this requirement by using appropriate phraseology in the opinion paragraph. Theoretically, the opinion could have been limited to fairness alone, but extending its coverage to generally accepted accounting principles accentuates the fact that conformity with these principles is necessary for achieving fairness of presentation.

The following discussion seeks to pinpoint some of the important concepts which enter into the meaning of the term *generally accepted* and underlie the auditor's use of judgment in determining whether management has fulfilled its responsibility to adhere to generally accepted accounting principles.

1. *Management's responsibilities.* The financial statements are the representations of management which has the full responsibility for their fairness of presentation and, therefore, for their conformity with generally accepted accounting principles.

2. *Auditor's responsibilities.* The auditor must comply with the first reporting standard. If the statements deviate from generally accepted accounting principles, he must disclose his qualifications and reservations and express either a qualified opinion or an adverse opinion.

3. *Auditor's influence.* When the auditor's examination reveals that the statements are not fair presentations in material respects, he is not expected to assume a passive role. It is the auditor's duty to explain fully to the client, and, when necessary, even to attempt to prove to him the nature and significance of the violations. The auditor can sometimes successfully influence a client to revise the accounts and the financial statements, thereby eliminating the qualifications. Management's adherence to generally accepted accounting principles is frequently achieved by its belief that a qualified or adverse opinion would affect unfavorably the company's relationship with credit grantors, stockholders, and other outside parties.

4. *Restrictions on arbitrary judgment.* The auditor may not, however, exercise his professional judgment in an arbitrary manner. He should not substitute his judgment for that of management when the latter has sound and reasonable support for its judgments. This note of caution is particularly applicable to sound accounting practices which entail using estimates, a knowledge of company and industry business practices, as well as the following considerations which necessarily provide for management a central role in the application of broad accounting principles to the particular circumstances of a company.

5. *Authoritative sources.* The reader may wish to refer to page

3 for a discussion of the bearing of authoritative sources on the determination of generally accepted accounting principles.

6. *Accounting principles and methods.* The term "generally accepted accounting principles" embraces not only the basic propositions and broad principles of accounting but also the accounting methods used in applying these principles. Both the principles and the methods used in their application must be generally accepted. For example, it is a broad, accepted principle that depreciable assets should be amortized over their useful lives. But if the particular depreciation method chosen by the company is not an acceptable method, the practice vitiates the principles. In other words, accounting principles cannot be separated from methods used in their application, and the two constitute an indivisible unit.

7. *Limited usage and general acceptance.* An accounting principle or method may have limited usage and still be generally accepted. An example of this is the units-of-production method or the sinking-fund method of computing depreciation.

8. *Diversity of practices.* A variety of generally accepted accounting methods may frequently be available in carrying out a broad accounting principle—for example, in computing depreciation or in providing for estimated losses on accounts receivable. In some instances, it is permissible to apply any one of these methods as an acceptable procedure regardless of the particular circumstances. In other instances, the method chosen must not only be generally accepted but a sound one and must be particularly applicable to the circumstances of the individual company. In still other instances, a unique method may be employed which is applicable to the industry or to the company but may be nevertheless regarded as "generally accepted" because it is sound in its achievement of fair and proper accounting results and in its implementation of a broad, generally accepted principle.

9. *Materiality.* A practice cannot be arbitrarily or mechanically characterized as unacceptable unless the essential factor of materiality is considered. A company, for example, may properly follow a consistent practice of expensing minor purchases of depreciable assets if the amounts, individually and in the aggregate, are not material.

10. *Estimates and uncertainties.* The financial statements, in many respects, reflect estimates and the existence of uncertainties rather than absolute fact and omniscience.

11. *Intention of management.* Management's intentions are an important element in the application of accounting principles. The in-

tention to sell assets previously held for long-term productive use or investment or to discontinue merchandise models or styles, for example, can materially affect the basis of valuation of such assets. The auditor's task in evaluating the propriety of accounting practice is often complicated by the difficulty in obtaining objective evidence that can effectively verify *intention*, which is, after all, essentially a subjective element.

12. *Regulated companies.* Statement on Auditing Procedure No. 33 makes it quite clear that the first reporting standard is fully applicable to the auditor's opinions on financial statements of public utilities, common carriers, insurance companies, financial institutions, and other such "regulated" companies. The accounting practices of such companies are prescribed by governmental regulatory agencies. The basic rules in this connection are as follows:

(a) *Accepted principles.* The broad, generally accepted accounting principles applicable to commercial organizations also apply in general to such regulated companies.

(b) *Differences.* There are differences, however, in the application of these principles. Some of these differences are the result of the rate-making process affecting regulated companies, whereas others may be imposed by the regulatory agency but may not necessarily conform with generally accepted accounting principles.

(c) *Effect of deviations.* When there are deviations from generally accepted accounting principles reflected in financial statements prepared for purposes other than filings with the regulatory agencies, the auditor must follow the usual reporting standards and express either a qualified or an adverse opinion.

(a) *Piecemeal opinion.* An adverse opinion may also be accompanied by a piecemeal opinion on parts of the statements or on any supplementary data not affected by the qualifications.

(e) *Opinion as to prescribed accounting.* When statements have been prepared in accordance with accounting regulations prescribed by the regulatory agency, and the auditor determines that he must submit a qualified opinion or an adverse opinion, he may at the request of the company express in addition an opinion that the financial statements conform with the prescribed accounting regulations.

It should be clear from the complexities cited in the foregoing discussion that the first reporting standard entails an expert knowledge by the auditor of generally accepted accounting principles and accounting methods, and the exercise of the highest type of professional judgment (ruling out arbitrariness and rigidity of viewpoint) in evaluating the soundness and relevance of their application to the circumstances of the individual company.

ACCOUNTING PRINCIPLES AND AUDITING PROCEDURES

Certain auditing procedures and approaches, such as those described below, are especially pertinent to the auditor's review of the propriety of the accounting principles, methods, and practices followed by the client. Some of these procedures are often undertaken by the company itself when the fairness with which a transaction is recorded is dependent upon a verification of underlying factors.

1. *Knowledge of company and industry practices.* Because the acceptability of an accounting practice, as previously explained, may depend on its applicability to the particular company or its industry, the auditor must acquire sufficient knowledge of their operating conditions and practices. This information is acquired by research on industry practices, observation, inquiries, review of the company's accounting policies and manuals, and, in general, in the process of performing the examination and reviewing the system of internal control.

2. *Discussion with management.* The propriety of the accounting methods is, in the first instance, the concern of management. It is therefore quite logical for the auditor, in doubtful circumstances, to place upon the client the responsibility of justifying its choice of method and of convincingly establishing the soundness of the accounting practice.

3. *Objective, verifiable evidence.* Because of the fundamental accounting concept that the data which enter into the accounting process are to be based on objective, verifiable evidence, it is incumbent upon the auditor to perform the following:

(a) Ascertain from the client, and also independently, the available evidential data which entered into the client's accounting judgments and estimates.

(b) Examine critically such data and evaluate their relative reliability and objectivity.

(c) Utilize such procedures as independent computation, overall evaluation, and independent inquiries, and apply the tests of logic, normality, inherent consistency, and reasonableness.

(d) Make an independent judgment concerning whether the evidential data support and are consistent with the accounting treatment in question.

(e) Form a conclusion as to the reasonableness, soundness, and propriety of the accounting practice involved.

4. *Consistency.* Consistency cannot be regarded as justification for an improper accounting practice; but in moments of doubt about accounting propriety, the auditor may look more favorably upon a particular accounting method or treatment if it has been consistently followed from year to year, on the theory that the financial statements and particularly earnings are stated on a comparable basis from year to year. To repeat, however, consistency cannot be used to condone a practice which is patently unacceptable and results in an unfair presentation of the balance sheet or income statement.

5. *Conservatism.* Conservatism enters into the auditor's thinking in two ways: he must determine whether the doctrine of conservatism has been properly applied by the company, and, when his judgments conflict with those of the company, he will usually adopt a conservative and cautious position in the light of his professional responsibilities to credit-grantors, stockholders, and outside parties.

6. *Orientation of management.* The financial condition of a company and its relationship with outside parties may sometimes orient management toward achieving certain accounting results. If, for example, the company is seeking a substantial loan or a loan renewal, certain accounting practices may be influenced by the desire to achieve a favorable financial presentation. These practices may range from simple optimism in estimates of, say, the allowances for bad debts and depreciation to the adoption of an unacceptable accounting practice. Although the independent accountant does not normally view management with suspicion in an invidious sense, he must, however, be alert to these possibilities. An awareness of the factors in the company's financial environment which may affect the client's orientation will certainly sharpen the auditor's focus in his review of the accounting practices.

CHAPTER *2*

REVENUE RECOGNITION AND MEASUREMENT

The final net income of a company is a computed figure which represents the difference between sales or other revenue and the sum of costs expired and expenses incurred during the accounting period. This chapter deals with the accounting principles governing the recognition and measurement of revenue. Chapter 3 is more directly concerned with costs and the basic concepts that distinguish unexpired cost, expired cost, expense, and loss.

MATCHING COSTS WITH REVENUE

As a computed figure, net income is arrived at by subtracting from revenue the expired costs, expenses, and losses incurred in earning such revenue. Costs must therefore be matched with the revenue to which they are applicable if the net income for an accounting period is to have any meaning. If revenue is reflected in one period and the applicable costs in another period, the net income for either period would not truly reflect the operating results.

The question, however, may be raised whether costs and expenses are first determined and then matched with related revenue or whether revenue is established first and then matched with the related costs and expenses.

Costs and expenses which are applicable to the production of future revenue are assets referred to as *unexpired costs*. These are held as assets until the realization of revenue. Once it is determined that revenue has been realized, these unexpired costs are then charged off as expired costs or expenses. Thus it is apparent that the first step in the matching process is to determine whether revenue has

56

been realized, and then to match appropriate costs with that revenue. In general, this is the pattern followed, but in some special circumstances involving particularly alternative practices in the recognition of revenue, such as for long-term construction-type contracts, the difficulties in estimating costs may entail a postponement of revenue recognition.

Losses are expired costs, but they differ from expenses in that they do not yield any benefit or advantage to the company. In other words, costs incurred which do not yield revenue may be viewed as losses and are therefore charged off in the period incurred obviously without regard to revenue matching.

PROCEEDS, REVENUE, INCOME—AICPA DEFINITIONS AND RECOMMENDATIONS

Accounting Terminology Bulletin No. 2 defines and makes recommendations, summarized below, for the proper use of the following terms: proceeds, revenue, income, profit, and earnings. All these terms except *proceeds* are related to changes in the capital or owners' equity resulting from a company's operations. The term *proceeds* differs from the others in that it refers to receipts, as from loans or capital contributions, and not from profit and loss transactions.

Proceeds

DEFINITION. This is a general term which refers to the total amount realized or received in a transaction such as a sale, issue of stock, collection of receivables, or borrowing of money.

RECOMMENDATION. As a general rule, the term *proceeds* should not be used as a caption in the basic financial statements. Its use should be confined to discussions of transactions. The bulletin limits the use of the term probably because readers of financial statements might mistakenly confuse the term with revenue.

Revenue

DEFINITION. (i) Revenue results from sale of goods or rendering of services; (ii) it is measured by the charge to customers, clients, etc., for goods or services furnished; (iii) it also includes gains from the sale or exchange of assets other than stock in trade, interest and dividends earned on investments, and increases in capital other than those resulting from capital contributions and capital adjustments like, for example, forgiveness of a debt.

DISCUSSION. Revenue is a gross concept like proceeds, but does not include collections from customers, receipts from loans, or owners' investments in the enterprise. For ordinary sales (that is, sales of merchandise inventory or of services), revenue is stated after deducting sales returns, allowances and discounts, freight, and similar items. In the case of other sales (for example, sales of fixed assets), revenue is stated after deducting the cost of assets sold (for example, a gain from sales or exchange). Revenue from ordinary sales, or from other transactions in the ordinary course of business, is sometimes described as *operating revenue.*

RECOMMENDATION. The above meaning of the term *revenue* should be adopted and used more widely in financial statements.

Income and Profit

DEFINITION. These two terms are *net* concepts and refer to the balances after the deduction from revenues of cost of goods sold, expenses, and losses, or only some of these items. The terms are often used synonymously and are often preceded by qualifying phrases such as *gross, operating, net,* etc.

DISCUSSION. The term *gross income* is often used as the equivalent of *revenue.* Public utilities may use the term *gross income* to describe the net income before deducting interest and other income charges. *Operating income* or *operating profit* is frequently used to describe the gross profit less ordinary expenses. *Net income* or *net profit* are terms used to designate the results of operations after deducting from revenues all related costs and expenses and all other expenses and losses applicable to the period. Of course, such deductions do not include dividends to stockholders or other such capital distributions.

RECOMMENDATION. (i) An appropriate qualifying adjective should precede the terms *income* or *profit.* (ii) *Gross income* should not be used as a substitute for items encompassed by the term *revenue.* (iii) The excess of operating revenue over cost of goods sold may be called *gross profit,* but it is better to use such terms as *gross profit on sales* or *gross margin.* (iv) The term *profit* may be used to describe a specific item such as profit on sale of fixed assets. (v) However, the following terms should be used in place of those noted parenthetically: operating income (operating profit); net income (net profit); income statement (statement of profit and loss).

Earnings

DEFINITION. The term *earnings* is often used synonymously with *net income,* particularly in referring to income over a period of years.

The phrase *earning power* refers to the demonstrated ability of a company to achieve earnings or net income.

RECOMMENDATION. The Committee states that between the use of *earnings* or *net income* it expresses no preference. It hopes that ultimately one of these terms may be uniformly adopted.

ACCOUNTING CONCEPT OF INCOME

Revenue is actually the amount of the inflow of assets received by the entity in an exchange transaction in which goods or services are given up by the entity. The transaction is one in which the enterprise hopes to achieve profits, that is, an excess of the amount of assets received over the amount of assets given up in exchange.

For the accountant, therefore, income is determined on the basis of specific transactions, and the increase in net assets for a specific accounting period attributable to profitable transactions is the arithmetical aggregate of individual transactional profits and losses. On the other hand, economists will often measure profits by referring to the value of an enterprise as a whole at the beginning and at the end of a period. Moreover, in arriving at the value of an enterprise's assets for this purpose, the asset values are regarded as equivalent to the sum of all future earnings to be derived from the asset, discounted for interest and other factors to their present worth.

Question—November 1963 (4a)

Much of accounting is concerned with the determination of income and the valuation of assets through the application of accounting principles and conventions. An example of the latter is the realization convention which controls the timing of revenue recognition; its influence is said to pervade both the income statement and the balance sheet. Explain the accounting concept of income.

Solution

1. *Transactions.* The accounting concept of income views profits as resulting from specific transactions entered into for profit-making purposes.

2. *Assets.* Income results in an increase in the net assets of the enterprise.

3. *Income versus capital.* The increase in net assets arising from

income must be clearly distinguished from an increase attributable to the contribution of capital by the owners or stockholders.

4. *Dealings in stock.* No gain or loss can result from any transaction which a corporation may have with respect to its own stock.

5. *Net concept.* Income is a net concept and represents the excess of assets received upon an exchange (revenue) over assets given up in the exchange (merchandise or other costs and expenses).

6. *Cost versus present value.* The costs considered by the accountant in computing income are the historical costs of the assets consumed (or given up) in the exchange and not their present value.

7. *Specific versus aggregate values.* Economists may measure profits by comparing the aggregate value of an enterprise at the end of a period with its beginning value. The values will have been determined by reference to the entity as a whole. Accountants, however, regard income as the arithmetic aggregate of profits and losses arising from individual business transactions.

REALIZATION CONVENTION

In the preceding chapter, the concept *value in exchange* was interpreted to mean that the assets of an entity are assigned values based upon the prices and money amounts as stated in exchange transactions consummated by the entity, occurring in an objective market. This is essentially what is meant by the term *realization convention*. In effect, revenue cannot be anticipated, and can be recorded only when an exchange has actually occurred.

Question—November 1963 (4b,c)

Discuss the realization convention and its significance to the process of periodic income determination.

Discuss the effect of the realization convention on the valuation of assets for balance sheet purposes.

Solution

Periodic Income

1. *Life of entity.* The income of an entity can be precisely determined only at the conclusion of its life and after its liquidation. At that time all the assets would be converted to cash, all liabilities paid, etc. Income would then represent the difference between the

cash originally contributed and the cash ultimately retained, with adjustments for items such as dividends and other distributions.

2. *Periodic income.* The needs of stockholders, management, creditors, and others require periodic reporting; hence the issuance of annual and other periodic statements.

3. *Estimates.* Because these periods are artificial and transactions and events frequently overlap from one period to the next, income determination must sometimes be based on estimates.

4. *Realization.* Revenue is recognized only when realized, that is, when received in a consummated exchange transaction. Revenue will ordinarily not be recognized with respect to a transaction that is uncompleted at the close of an accounting period.

5. *Objectivity.* The requirement with respect to a consummated exchange transaction insures revenue recognition only upon an objective basis. In the absence of objective and verifiable evidence that revenue has been achieved, subjectivity and arbitrary estimates would determine the income to be recorded.

6. *Timing of recognition.* Although productive and other efforts precede the ultimate exchange transaction, revenue is recognized only upon the occasion of the transaction and not when the original effort was expended. Thus, no income is recognized as merchandise is manufactured and completed; an actual sale must take place for the realization convention to be operative.

Valuation of Assets

1. *Allocation versus valuation.* Accounting is a process of allocation and not of valuation. This statement has applicability to productive assets such as merchandise and fixed assets and means that asset values on the balance sheet represent the residue remaining after appropriate costs for the accounting period have been charged off against revenue.

2. *Income versus balance sheet.* The focus in accounting is upon the proper determination of net income, rather than upon the valuation of assets for balance sheet purposes. The latter does constitute a matter of concern to the accountant, but the emphasis is a secondary one.

3. *Deferred costs.* Assets therefore may be largely considered to be in the nature of deferred costs awaiting a write-off to income in future periods.

4. *Unrealized income.* Until income is realized, expenditures made for production of income represent deferred costs to be carried as assets.

5. *Deductions from revenue.* Although revenue is a gross concept, the corresponding receivables from customers are stated after deduction of appropriate allowances for discounts, sales, etc. The theory is that the authentic asset received in the exchange is not really the gross receivable but the amount to be ultimately collected.

TIMING OF REVENUE RECOGNITION

Revenue is considered to be realized when, as stated in ARB No. 43, Chapter 1, "a sale in the ordinary course of business is effected, unless the circumstances are such that the collection of the sale price is not reasonably assured." Other bases could, however, have been selected by accounting for the timing of revenue recognition if it were willing to compromise with criteria of objectivity, certainty, and conservatism. The following is a listing of various points at which revenue might conceivably be considered to be realized, together with a significant pro and con argument for each.

1. *Acquisition of productive asset.* (*Pro*) If merchandise or other assets have been acquired at a bargain price, revenue should be recognized. (*Con*) Profits are made not through the act of buying, but through productive utilization of acquired assets.

2. *Holding gains—appreciation of assets.* (*Pro*) If assets acquired for productive use increase in value during the period they are so held, such holding gains—measured in terms of either replacement values or selling prices—are real economic gains and should be recognized. (*Con*) Such recognition would violate the historical cost basis of accounting for assets. Any alleged economic gain will be reflected in the ultimate selling price.

3. *Manufacturing.* (*Pro*) Revenue should be earned in accordance with the amount of productive effort expended, on the theory that accomplishment (revenue) can be achieved only through effort (cost incurred).(*Con*) There is too great a degree of uncertainty regarding the ultimate sale and selling price.

4. *Accretion.* (*Pro*) Revenue arises from accretion of assets such as growing timber, livestock, and aging of liquor. The increase in quantity or quality goes hand-in-hand with a corresponding increase in asset value. (*Con*) The accretion process should be looked upon as the equivalent of the manufacturing process and similarly cannot be accepted as the time for revenue recognition.

5. *Finished goods.* (*Pro*) Revenue should be recorded at the com-

pletion of the manufacturing cycle, on the basis of the estimated selling prices of the finished goods since little more remains except to make an actual sale. (*Con*) Revenue cannot be recorded except upon a consummated exchange transaction.

6. *Customer order.* (*Pro*) Revenue should be recognized when a sales order has been received and accepted because at that point a legal contract is in effect. (*Con*) It is only the actual passage of title that signalizes the completed transaction and the full legal significance of an executed, rather than executory, contract.

7. *Sale.* (*Pro*) The point of sale when title to merchandise has actually passed is the acceptable basis for recording revenue. It meets the required standards of objectivity, certainty, and conservatism. (*Con*) Income can be arbitrarily manipulated between accounting periods by the simple timing of the sale.

8. *Collection.* (*Pro*) Revenue should be recognized only to the extent of the cash collected since any receivable may not ultimately be collected in full. (*Con*) This basis is too conservative and, moreover, overlooks the provision which can be made for estimated discounts, returns, and bad debts.

SALES BASIS FOR REVENUE RECOGNITION

With very few exceptions, the point of sale is the method of recognizing revenue which conforms with generally accepted accounting principles.

Question—May 1965 (3a,b)

Revenue is usually recognized at the point of sale. Under special circumstances, however, bases other than the point of sale are used for the timing of revenue recognition.

(a) Why is the point of sale usually used as the basis for the timing of revenue recognition?

(b) Disregarding the special circumstances when bases other than the point of sale are used, discuss the merits of each of the following objections to the sales basis of revenue recognition:

(i) It is too conservative because revenue is earned throughout the entire process of production.

(ii) It is not conservative enough because accounts receivable do not represent disposable funds, sales returns and allowances may be made, and collection and bad debt expenses may be incurred in a later period.

Solution

Justification for Point of Sale

1. *Objectivity.* The actual sale is the basis for revenue recognition which conforms most fully with the standard of objectivity. Subjectivity with respect to price, consummation of a transaction, and other such factors is reduced to a minimum.

2. *Exchange transaction.* The exchange transaction fixes a clearcut and objective point for revenue recognition.

3. *Arms-length transaction.* The fact that the transaction must be at arms length ensures the element of objectivity.

4. *Objective, verifiable evidence.* An exchange transaction is a real economic event and, as such, yields evidence in written and oral form which ensures objectivity and verifiability of the event.

5. *Costs.* Since the sale has presumably taken place only after the product is ready for sale or the service has actually been rendered, substantially all related costs will have been incurred and become known. Hence the matching of cost and revenue will have been considerably facilitated.

6. *Legality.* The sale is the point at which the contract has been executed and the legal rights of the seller realized. Thus an enforceable claim arises which, to that extent, ensures the collectibility of the receivable.

Selected Objections

1. *Conservatism.* It is true that the sales basis represents a postponement of revenue relative to the production basis and, to that extent, may be viewed as being too conservative. However, the production basis would recognize and anticipate revenue before it has actually been realized.

2. *Effort and accomplishment.* It would be desirable to accrue revenue throughout the entire process of production because revenue would then be directly matched with productive effort. The following, however, are some of the uncertainties which do not make it feasible to relate revenue to production: stage of completion of merchandise; measurement of increased value; salability of merchandise; cost to complete.

3. *Disposable funds.* It would not be correct to say that the sales basis is not conservative enough because the full receivable may not be collected. Appropriate accruals can be made as of the balance sheet date for sales returns and allowances, discounts, and bad debts.

4. *Estimates.* Although the accruals for such deductions from revenue would have to be made on an estimated basis, this factor does not militate against the sales basis of accounting for revenue. Estimates made on a systematic, reasonable, and rational basis fully conform with generally accepted accounting practice.

INSTALLMENT BASIS OF ACCOUNTING

The installment basis of accounting views revenue as earned not at the point of sale but as cash is collected from customers. Each installment payment is regarded as consisting of a recovery of cost and, to the extent of the gross profit percentage applied to the collection, a realization of profit.

Question—November 1965 (3a)

Installment sales usually are accounted for by one of the following methods: (1) the profit may be recognized as earned in the period of sale; (2) the profit may be recognized on a proportionate basis in the periods of collection (commonly called the "installment method").

Discuss the propriety of the two methods, including in your discussion a list of the circumstances under which recognition of profit in the period of sale would be preferable to recognition of profit on the installment method.

Solution

(The propriety of the sales basis of accounting is discussed on page 64 in the solution to Question—May 1965 (3a,b).)

In the following discussion of the propriety of the installment basis of accounting for installment sales, the argument in favor (*pro*) will be presented first, followed by a counter argument (*con*).

1. *Cash basis.* (*Pro*) No revenue is actually realized until cash assets are received. (*Con*) The usual method of accounting is the accrual basis which recognizes assets other than cash, such as customers' receivables, accrued liabilities, etc.

2. *Collectibility.* (*Pro*) Because of the greater credit risk associated with customers who purchase on the installment plan, the full selling price may not be ultimately collected. It would therefore

be improper to pick up the entire profit at point of sale. (*Con*) An appropriate allowance for bad debts could be recorded to reflect the credit standing of the customers.

3. *Long-term receivables.* (*Pro*) The long period of collection is an additional factor affecting the ultimate collectibility of the full receivable. The longer the period of collection, the greater are the uncertainties that are introduced. (*Con*) Here, too, an estimated allowance for bad debts can be recorded. Moreover, the seller can repossess the property if necessary.

4. *Asset realization.* (*Pro*) A considerable time must elapse before the selling price is fully realized in cash. The long-term receivables in themselves do not provide real working capital. (*Con*) Working capital can be increased simply by borrowing against the receivables.

5. *Future effort.* (*Pro*) The deferral of revenue recognition to later periods is especially justified because of the long period of future collection efforts entailing protracted bookkeeping and customer contacts. (*Con*) The bookkeeping and collection efforts may not necessarily exceed those required for regular sales. In any event, they can be treated as period costs.

6. *After-costs.* (*Pro*) Billing, collection, and bookkeeping costs which arise after the actual sale are higher than for regular sales. Revenue should therefore be deferred as in the installment basis so that such after-costs may be matched with revenue. (*Con*) Such matching could be achieved by accruing estimated after-costs.

7. *Taxes.* (*Pro*) There is a tax deferral benefit if the company uses the installment method for tax purposes. (*Con*) The use of the installment method for tax purposes does not require its similar use for general accounting purposes.

8. *Conservatism.* (*Pro*) The installment basis, by recording revenue on a pro rata basis in accordance with collections, is more conservative than the sales basis which picks up income in full at the time of sale. (*Con*) Such undue conservatism is not warranted. Moreover, the installment method is itself not as conservative as the cost recovery method by which no income is recorded until cash collections exceed the cost.

9. *Recordkeeping.* (*Pro*) The maintenance of records which account separately for installment and regular sales and expenses is of help to management in formulating policies and controls. (*Con*) The cost of such recordkeeping can become burdensome, especially in view of the difficulties which can sometimes exist in relating collections to the year of sale and the appropriate gross profit.

LONG-TERM CONSTRUCTION-TYPE CONTRACTS

The following discussion summarizes the accounting principles governing the recognition of revenue for long-term construction-type contracts as set forth in Accounting Research Bulletin No. 45.

Question—November 1953 (9)

State and explain the considerations involved in deciding whether a general contractor should take up revenue on the "completed contracts" basis or on the "percentage of completion" basis.

Solution

Percentage-of-completion Method

1. *Calculation.* Under the percentage-of-completion method, income is recognized by applying to the estimated total income a percentage factor representing either (a) the proportion that costs to date bear to estimated total costs or (b) some other appropriate relationship of work completed to total work to be performed.

2. *Extent of completion.* Costs incurred during the early stages, as for materials, might have to be adjusted for purposes of percentage calculation if such costs do not clearly correspond to the stage of completion.

3. *Advantages.* The advantages of this method are as follows:

(a) Income is recognized periodically as work progresses rather than at the completion of the contract.

(b) Effort is thereby more closely matched with revenue.

(c) The profitability of uncompleted contracts is more clearly ascertained in view of the estimates which must be made of costs to complete.

4. *Disadvantages.* The principal disadvantage of the percentage-of-completion method is the uncertainty with respect to estimates of future costs, stage of completion, percentage of completion, and, where applicable, lack of a firm contract price.

5. *Passage of title.* The question may be raised as to the acceptability of this method since, under the usual circumstances of sale of merchandise, revenue is not recorded until the passage of title to the customer. A long-term construction-type contract should not

however, be viewed as a sale of merchandise. It can be regarded as the offering of services, rather than goods, to the customer and, hence, as "service income" that can be accrued periodically. Moreover, the costs incurred by the contractor can be regarded as the customer's "property" for which reimbursement is to be made.

6. *Provision for losses.* If the estimates of total contract cost suggest that a loss will be realized on the entire contract, a provision for the full loss must be recorded as soon as determined. Losses cannot be postponed to future periods.

7. *Preferred method.* When estimates of cost to complete and the stage of completion can be fairly accurately determined, and when the contract price is firm and collectibility is not in question, the percentage-of-completion method is preferable to the completed-contract method.

Completed-contract Method

8. *Calculation.* According to the completed-contract method, income is recognized only when the contract is substantially completed. At that time all costs are known as well as, of course, the contract price.

9. *General and administrative expenses.* Such expenses may be appropriately treated as deferred costs awaiting the completion of the contract, rather than as charges to periodic income. Such deferral is particularly desirable when there are few contracts and completion dates and contract profits are irregular and uneven.

10. *Advantages.* The major advantage of this method is that the operating results are definitely known before revenue is recorded. It becomes unnecessary to deal with uncertainties and estimates pertaining to stage of completion and future costs.

11. *Disadvantages.* This method can result in an irregular recognition of income and in the failure to properly match periodic effort and income.

12. *Losses.* Provision should be made for all foreseeable losses which should be recorded when determined and not deferred to the completion of the contract.

SALES DISCOUNTS AND SIMILAR REVENUE DEDUCTIONS

Revenue is a gross concept and corresponds to the assets received in an exchange transaction. However, because the perspective is directed toward the ultimate realization of these assets in cash, revenue is stated after deduction of sales returns, allowances, discounts, and, in some instances, freight.

Question—May 1956 (10)

In an audit of the accounts of the ABC Company, you find an account *Allowance for Cash Discount on Sales* with a credit balance of $4,000.

(a) What is the nature of this account? Under what conditions would you assume that the account would be charged and/or credited?

(b) How would this account be classified in the financial statements? Why?

(c) What is the theoretical justification for using the procedure followed by the ABC Company? Give any objections to the procedure which you see.

Solution

Nature of Account

This account was created by an offsetting charge to Sales Discounts, based upon the estimated discounts to be granted after the balance sheet date relative to receivables outstanding at that date. Depending upon the bookkeeping system in use, the account could either be closed out by reversal entry in the month following the statement date or, alternatively, retained on the books but subject to debit or credit adjustments at the end of a subsequent period.

Classification

The allowance account should be presented as an offset against Accounts Receivable in the same manner as the allowance for bad debts, returns, and similar valuation accounts. This reduction corresponds to the amount that will not be collected in cash.

Justification and Objections

1. *Revenue measurement.* The allowance serves to measure the amount of revenue received in terms of the ultimate cash to be collected, and similarly reduces the asset to the amount expected to be collected.

2. *Revenue reduction.* The reduction of the asset on the balance sheet will have its counterpart in the deduction of sales discounts from sales on the statement of income.

3. *Income determination.* Although sales discounts are more in the nature of direct deductions in arriving at revenue rather than costs to be matched with revenue, the accrual of sales discounts may still be viewed as a means of achieving a fairer determination of net income. In this way all discounts applicable to the period's sales will have been provided for.

4. *Recurring item.* The objection may be made that since the amount of sales discounts provided for in the accrual recurs from year to year, there is no need to make such provision. The periodic income statement would remain comparable. This objection would be valid providing the amount of the accrual remains the same from year to year. However, in the absence of accrual, the receivables would be overstated.

5. *Immateriality.* Objection to the accrual can also be made on the ground that the amount accrued would usually be immaterial and therefore have little effect on income. However, the degree of materiality in this regard would depend on the individual company and circumstances.

6. *Estimates.* The fact that the accrual is based on estimates can be offered as an objection, but this would overlook the frequent use of estimates and approximations in arriving at accounting accruals. Moreover, by a review of the collections in the subsequent period, a relatively precise determination of discounts could be obtained.

7. *Sales verus collection.* The sales discounts applicable to outstanding receivables and actually granted in the subsequent period, can be regarded as a charge to income attributable to the collection experience of the subsequent period rather than to the sales of the prior period.

BAD DEBTS—REVENUE DEDUCTION VERSUS EXPENSE

Bad debts expense is properly classified on the income statement as an operating expense, but the question is sometimes raised as to whether it would not be more appropriate to present it as a deduction from sales—that is, as a deduction in arriving at revenue.

Question—May 1953 (1c)

Bad debts expense may be classified in the income statements as a direct deduction from Sales. Give the theoretical justification for such treatment.

Solution

1. *Revenue deduction.* Revenue is a gross concept but is generally stated after deducting returns, allowances, discounts, and similar items. Bad debts can be viewed as an example of such similar items.

2. *Allowance for bad debts.* Since the allowance account is presented as a deduction from accounts receivable, bad debts expense should similarly be shown as a deduction from sales.

3. *Cash realization.* Revenue represents the assets received in exchange for goods or services rendered, but these assets are expressed with reference to their cash equivalence. Hence, discounts are deducted from sales in arriving at net sales and it is the latter figure which constitutes revenue. By the same token, it could be argued that bad debts should be deducted from sales to show net sales in accordance with the cash which will ultimately be received.

4. *Cash outlay.* An expense usually originates as an expenditure ultimately involving an outlay of cash. However, bad debts take the form not of a cash outlay, but of the failure to receive an expected amount of cash.

5. *Operating expense.* The generally accepted practice is to treat bad debts as an operating expense rather than as a deduction from sales. The justification for this practice is that the gross amount charged originally to accounts receivable represents the proper measure of asset value, and that any expected losses are in the nature of expenses to be matched against revenue. Treating bad debts as an expense in this fashion reflects the view that bad debts are an inherent part of credit-selling operations. The counter-argument is that bad debts represents an adjustment to originally recorded revenue, rather than a cost incurred in order to produce revenue.

ACCOUNTING FOR BAD DEBTS

The two commonly known methods of accounting for bad debts are the allowance method (sometimes referred to as the accrual method) and the write-off method (under which bad debts expense is charged only when an actual bad debt has occurred).

Question—November 1964 (2a)

During the audit of accounts receivable, your client asks why the current year's expense for bad debts is charged merely because some accounts may become uncollectible next year. He then said that he had read that financial statements should be based upon verifiable, objective evidence, and that it seemed to him to be much more objective to wait until individual accounts receivable were actually determined to be uncollectible before charging them to expense.

1. Discuss the theoretical justification of the allowance as contrasted with the direct write-off method of accounting for bad debts.

2. Describe the following two methods of estimating bad debts. Include a discussion of how well each accomplishes the objectives of the allowance method of accounting for bad debts.

    (a) The percentage of sales method.

    (b) The aging method.

3. Of what merit is your client's contention that the allowance method lacks the objectivity of the direct write-off method? Discuss in terms of accounting's measurement function.

Solution

Justification of Allowance Method

1. *Income statement.* The allowance method achieves a fairer figure for net income because the expense is charged against the related sales rather than against unrelated revenue of subsequent periods.

2. *Matching cost and revenue.* Even if the estimated bad debts charged to income is not viewed as being related to the *revenue* (sales) of the particular period, the expense can, nevertheless, be said to be a period charge to be deducted in arriving at *income* for the period.

3. *Systematic charges.* The write-off method would result in irregular charges to income, and the amounts would vary considerably from period to period. The allowance method results in systematic charges to income.

4. *Balance sheet.* The allowance method serves to present fairly the accounts receivable at their estimated realizable value.

Percentage of Sales Method

1. *Calculation.* Keyed as this method is to sales, the emphasis is on the charge to bad debts expense rather than on the periodic adjustment of the allowance for bad debts account. Thus, in each year or other accounting period, an appropriate percentage is applied to the period's credit (sometimes total) sales and the resulting amount is charged to bad debts expense.

2. *Rate.* The percentage rate used is one that takes into consideration credit policy, past experience, and other relevant data.

3. *Income determination.* The focus in this method is on the proper determination of income and on the matching of cost and revenue, rather than on the valuation of accounts receivable.

4. *Balance sheet.* Although it is true that the balance sheet has only secondary importance in this respect, the allowance account does have the effect of reducing the gross receivable in some appropriate measure to their realizable value.

5. *Cumulative effect.* Inasmuch as the percentage method involves continual additions to the allowance (offset, of course, by actual write-offs), in time the balance in the allowance for bad debts account may be substantially out of proportion to the accounts receivable balance and to possible future bad debt losses. This distortion can be cured, however, by appropriate adjustments in the rate or otherwise as circumstances may suggest.

Aging Method

1. *Calculation.* The aging method entails an analysis of the composition of accounts receivable by age—that is, the period of time elapsed since the date of sale, or due date for collection. Based on such an analysis, an amount of estimated bad debts is calculated, and it is that amount at which the allowance account is stated. The charge to income corresponds to that amount necessary to increase the allowance account to the required figure. Calculations may be based on different percentage rates applied to the various age categories. Where appropriate, estimates may be based on an evaluation of individual accounts.

2. *Balance sheet.* This method emphasizes the balance sheet and the reporting of receivables at their realizable value.

3. *Income statement.* This method does have the effect, despite its balance sheet emphasis, of providing for periodic charges to income for bad debts expense. This matching of expense and income is not as accurate, however, as that achieved by the percentage method, which clearly relates the expense charge to revenue volume for the period.

4. *Allocation verus valuation.* The percentage method is more clearly representative of the basic concept that accounting is a process of allocation and not of valuation. The aging method is indicative of a concern with balance sheet valuation.

Objective Evidence

1. *Objectivity as a relative concept.* The accounting concept of objectivity does not require that a choice be made of that accounting method which is the most objective. Objectivity is a relative concept, and the degree of objectivity required in accounting measurements may depend on whether we are dealing with revenue recognition, cost expiration, etc.

2. *Revenue versus expense and losses.* Revenue is recognized only when it has materialized in an objective exchange market. Expenses and losses, however, are recorded on the basis of estimates and of reasonable judgment as to their occurrence.

3. *Estimates, certainty, and objectivity.* Even though the allowance method is based on estimates, there are objective guides which can be used in making such estimates—for example, past experience, industry collection data, credit reports, etc. Thus the concept of objectivity can be applied in circumstances which contain elements of certainty or uncertainty. It would be improper to wait until a loss or expense has materialized before an appropriate estimated accrual is made.

4. *Uncollectibility.* Subjective considerations may be present even in the use of a seemingly completely objective method like the direct write-off method. It is often difficult to determine when an account is actually uncollectible.

5. *Sales and bad debts—consistency of method.* An even more objective method of recording sales could have been the cash basis. No question could then exist regarding ultimate realization of revenue in cash. The company, however, chose to be on the accrual basis for sales, in conformity with generally accepted accounting principles. It is therefore consistent with that practice to also account for bad debts on an accrual basis.

CHAPTER **3**

COST AND COST EXPIRATION

ASSETS, COST, AND INCOME DETERMINATION

Assets generally emerge in one of three ways: (1) as cash proceeds in the form of loans or investments of stockholders, proprietors, or creditors; (2) as cash or accounts receivable resulting from revenue transactions; or (3) as goods or services acquired by purchase to be used for the production of income. Broadly, therefore, there are two types of assets: monetary assets such as cash, receivables, and marketable securities which are the end result and goal of a company's productive efforts; and productive assets which are held for the production of future revenue.

Accounting Terminology Bulletin No. 1 defines an asset as an expenditure which is a property right or value properly applicable to the future. The following is a more comprehensive statement of the characteristics which assets have in general and of the properties which may vary with type of asset.

1. *Value.* An asset is something of economic value.
2. *Money.* The value must be expressible in terms of money.
3. *Right.* The accounting entity must have the right to the use or benefits of the asset for the purposes for which it was acquired.
4. *Nature of right.* The right may take various forms.

(a) *Ownership.* In some cases, such as the purchase of machinery, inventories, and security investments, the right rests upon legal ownership.

(b) *Claim to services.* In other instances, as in the case of insurance, interest, and wages, the right is based on a claim to services arising out of a contract.

(c) *Claim to other assets.* Other assets, such as receivables, possess the characteristic of a right in the form of a legal claim to other assets, usually cash.

(d) *Privilege.* The right may take the form of a privilege, such as a patent, franchise, or copyright granted by a governmental agency, or a privilege arising out of contract with a private party. An example of the latter is the right given a tenant to install leasehold improvements and to use the latter for appropriate purposes during the period of tenancy.

5. *Conditions and restrictions.* The right must be unconditional with respect to use or benefits for which the asset was intended. If the property is owned, it is *ipso facto* unrestricted in use. If the right takes any other form—such as a claim to services, privileges or cash—any restrictions on the *intended* use or benefits will, to the extent of such conditions, detract from the asset character of the item.

6. *Time element—present value.* The value of an asset is affected by considerations of time. Thus a long-term receivable which bears no interest may be regarded as having a utility equivalent only to its *present value* (that is, the gross amount discounted to the present for interest and time). However, adjustments of this type are not in conformity with generally accepted accounting principles unless there is clear evidence that the sales price includes a financing or interest charge. The more prevalent practice is to make such an adjustment to record the asset at the value equivalent to cash cost in appropriate cases of productive assets acquired on a long-term payment basis.

7. *Tangible and intangible.* Since an asset is a right which has economic value, it may be tangible or intangible. The intuitive feeling of some that a tangible asset has greater value than an intangible asset because of its material substance runs counter to the definition of an asset. Intangible assets have value because of their utility, which may be greater or less than the benefits which tangible assets are expected to yield.

8. *Utility.* Utility is an essential characteristic of an asset. Some assets, such as fixed assets and inventories, derive their utility from their applicability to the production of future revenue. Other assets, like cash or receivables, have unusual utility in that they can be used for any business purpose.

9. *Utility to the entity.* The utility of an asset is judged in relation to the specific entity. What may be considered useful for one entity and thus treated as an asset may be viewed by another as worthless and, therefore, a loss.

COST, EXPENSE AND LOSS

Although the term *cost* is frequently regarded as being similar to an expense and therefore associated with the income statement, a more advanced interpretation of its meaning would regard all costs as assets, at least initially and tentatively until they have expired and lost their utility. Accounting Terminology Bulletin No. 4, entitled *Cost, Expense, and Loss*, develops the distinctions between these terms.

Question—November 1955 (7a)

State the theoretical distinction between *costs* and *expenses* and *losses* in a corporation engaged in manufacturing. Explain the possible differences in the accounting treatment of expenses and losses.

Solution

1. *Cost.* This is the amount expended for goods or services received or to be received. The expenditure may have been in cash or the money equivalent of other property given up, services performed, capital stock issued, or liability incurred.

2. *Unexpired costs.* These are assets which are useful in the production of future revenue. Inventories, prepaid expenses, plant, investments, and deferred charges are examples of unexpired costs.

3. *Expired costs.* When unexpired costs are no longer useful for the production of income, they may be said to have expired and are then treated as deductions on the income statement or, when extraordinary and in accordance with certain principles, on the statement of retained earnings. Current expenses and costs of products or assets sold are examples of expired costs. A loss is also an expired cost to the extent that the cost exceeds the proceeds received on disposition of assets.

4. *Transferability of unexpired costs.* Unexpired costs can be transferred from one asset classification to another before final expiration. Thus part of the cost of plant or unexpired insurance may become incorporated in inventories to the extent that the valuation of inventories includes an allocable portion of such overhead items as depreciation and insurance on plant. When inventories are sold, the asset becomes an expired cost along with the transferred costs.

5. *Expense.* In the broad sense, expense includes all expired costs deducted from revenues, including cost of sales, operating expenses,

and losses on sale of property. The narrower use of the term restricts it to operating, selling, and administrative expenses, including interest and taxes, usually referred to as period costs. Period costs are distinguished from product costs which are the costs of acquisition or manufacture of merchandise inventories. Whereas product costs can be directly matched with specific revenue, period costs are considered to have expired on the basis of time and are charged to income of the period in which incurred.

As a matter of convenience in recordkeeping, expenses (and some costs) may be recorded immediately in expense accounts as deductions from income. At the time of preparation of the financial statements, adjustments may be made to record the unexpired amounts as prepaid expenses. These expenses could just as well have been initially recorded as assets, that is, as prepaid expenses subject to later adjustment and write-off of the appropriate portion as "expired" expenses. It is in this sense that even fixed asset costs may be referred to as prepaid expenses.

6. *Loss.* This term may be viewed in several ways: (a) as the excess of all expenses (in the broad connotation) over revenues, that is, as *net loss* for the period; or (b) the excess of cost over proceeds of assets sold, abandoned, destroyed, or otherwise written off; or (c) in general, expenditures for which corresponding benefits are not received.

Whereas expenses represent beneficial costs, losses signify the lack of benefit. Therefore, although expenses, if unexpired, can be deferred as assets, losses must be written off immediately when known to have occurred.

7. *Extraordinary verus recurring items.* Expenses are usually of a recurring nature and are viewed as normal deductions from income. Losses are frequently extraordinary, nonrecurring, and unexpected. Although expenses are presented in the statement of income in view of their identification with the usual or typical operations of the business, material extraordinary losses are carried directly to retained earnings if their inclusion in income would tend to make the income statement misleading.

8. *Statement terminology—cost.* The term *cost* may be appropriately used on the balance sheet when noting the basis of asset valuation or in the income statement in referring to *cost* of goods sold or cost of other properties or investments sold or written off. Expenses such as material, labor, and overhead entering into cost of manufacturing should be referred to as *costs*.

9. *Statement terminology—expense.* This term should be used on

the income statement only in the narrower sense for operating expenses.

10. *Statement terminology—loss.* This term should be used to describe net results (for example, net loss from operations, etc.) or the results of specific transactions (for example, loss on sale of fixed assets).

TERMINOLOGY FOR COST AND EXPENSE—ILLUSTRATIVE PROBLEM

Many of the ways in which the terms *cost* and *expense* are actually used in financial statements do not conform with the rules expressed in the accounting terminology bulletin, as illustrated in the following case situation.

Question—May 1959 (5)

Mr. Brown recently purchased some shares of stock in the Lalow Manufacturing Company, and is very interested in the annual report to the stockholders which he has just received. He is confused by the use of the terms *expense* and *cost* found throughout the statements in this report, and has asked you to distinguish for him what accountants mean by the words *expense* and *cost* and how they can be used in so many places throughout the statements. The specific items which he questions are:

In the balance sheet: (a) organization expense, and (b) a footnote, stating that plant machinery and equipment includes "installation expenses" of $40,000.

In the *cost of goods manufactured and sold* statement: a classification "manufacturing expenses" with various items under this heading which include the term *expense.* You are to:

(a) Distinguish between the terms *expense* and *cost.*

(b) State how each of the items mentioned by Mr. Brown "fits" your definition. If you think any of these items are improperly called *expenses,* indicate why and suggest more appropriate terminology.

Solution

1. *Cost and expense.* For the solution to part (a) see Question—November 1955 (7a), page 77.

2. *Organization expense.* This is an asset account appearing on the balance sheet, but the terminology, which is quite conventional,

creates the impression that it is an expense. The term *organization costs* would be an improvement, but it could still be misconstrued as a profit and loss item. A better term, but one not commonly used, might be *unamortized* (or *deferred*) *organization costs*. If this asset is, in fact, amortized on some systematic basis, the periodic amount so charged-off may be appropriately presented in the statement of income as *organization expense* or *amortization of organization costs*. In general, it is inappropriate to use the term *expense* on the balance sheet unless it is modified by suitable phraseology such as *prepaid insurance expense* or *unamortized bond discount and expense*, which enables the reader to identify the item as an asset.

3. *Installation expenses.* These expenditures are part of the total cost of acquiring the fixed assets and placing them in a condition for use. They are, therefore, assets and not expenses. It is unnecessary to disclose the component elements of asset costs. Installation costs are just as much a part of the total asset cost as the purchase price. If such disclosure is necessary, a better term would be *installation costs*.

4. *Manufacturing expenses.* Accounting Terminology Bulletin No. 4 states that items entering into cost of manufacturing, such as material, labor, and overhead, should be described as costs and not as expenses. Until the manufactured products are sold, these items are unexpired costs and, as assets, are transferable to another asset—inventories. These manufacturing costs become expired costs or expenses to the extent that they are allocated to cost of goods sold.

PRODUCTIVE ASSETS AND RELATIONSHIP TO FUTURE REVENUE

Productive assets derive their utility from the fact that they have applicability to future revenue. The major productive assets (unexpired costs) are inventories, fixed assets, certain deferred charges such as research and development costs, and intangible assets. The following is a discussion of several of the major categories by which the relationship of such assets to future revenue may be classified.

1. *Direct relationship to specific future revenue.* Unexpired costs which are most easily recognized as assets are those which can be directly related to the specific future revenue which will result from the sale of these assets. They are such direct generators of revenue that their utility is unmistakable. Examples are accumulated costs on construction-type contracts, merchandise inventories in general, and security investments.

2. *Potential direct relationship to specific future revenue.* Certain assets which are depreciable or amortizable have both a potential and direct relationship to future revenue. The portion of such costs which has been applied to production may become attached to other costs which are directly related to specific future revenue. The remaining cost may be said to have a *potential* direct relationship to specific future revenue. Examples are fixed assets used in manufacturing and prepaid insurance relating to plant. Thus machinery and equipment are unexpired costs which will, in the future, be allocated to the production of inventories. The depreciation charged off during a certain period is transferred as an unexpired cost to the accumulated inventory costs, which in turn have the status of unexpired costs until sold. The depreciation charges thereby become directly related to the future revenue specifically derivable from the inventories. The undepreciated balance of the fixed assets will, in the future, be identified with costs applicable to specific revenue.

3. *Direct relationship to nonspecific future revenue.* Certain expenditures may be directly related to the production of future revenue in general, although it may be difficult or impossible to associate the specific costs with specific income. Examples are prepaid advertising, especially institutional advertising, and patents covering production processes.

4. *General relationship to future operations.* The utility of many unexpired costs lies in the fact that they relate to future operations in general although the benefits of these expenditures cannot be specifically identified with future revenue. Examples are prepaid expenses or fixed assets which will be charged off to administrative and general overhead expenses, and franchises.

5. *Relationship to corporate existence.* The farthest removed from precise identification with future income are those assets, referred to as organization expenses, whose incurrence was necessary in order to bring the entity into existence. Since the existence of the entity is the precondition for any of its activities, such assets derive their utility from their relationship to the total and overall activities of the enterprise extending into the indefinite future.

MERCHANDISE INVENTORIES

A comprehensive discussion of the general principles applicable to inventory valuation may be found in ARB No. 43, Chapter 4. Certain sections of Accounting Terminology Bulletin No. 4 are also perti-

nent. The following is an interpretive summary of accounting principles and rules relating to merchandise inventories as set forth in these
pronouncements.

Definition of Inventories

1. *General.* Inventories are goods held for sale in the ordinary
course of business (including finished goods of a manufacturer), work
in process, and raw materials and supplies which are to be consumed
directly or indirectly in the production of goods or services to be
available for sale.

2. *Exclusions.* Inventories do not include long-term depreciable
assets or goods which will be so used, nor does the term embrace
depreciable assets retired from productive use and held for sale.

3. *Inclusions.* But raw materials and supplies which may be consumed for the construction of long-term assets or other such purposes
need not be separately classified if they constitute a small proportion
of total inventories. Some companies, such as oil producers, by trade
practice usually treat operating materials and supplies as inventory.

Objective of Accounting for Inventories

1. *Revenues.* Inventories are financially significant because of the
revenues obtainable from the sale of goods or services where production
entails the use of inventories.

2. *Matching cost and revenue.* The major objective is the matching of appropriate costs with revenue so that income may be properly
determined.

3. *Unexpired cost.* The inventory on hand at any date is the balance of unexpired cost remaining after the matching of expired costs
with related revenue.

4. *Future cost.* The unexpired cost is carried forward as an asset
to subsequent periods to become a future expired cost; but the amount
carried forward cannot exceed the amount that may properly be
matched against future revenues.

Basis of Accounting

1. *Cost.* Since accounting in general is primarily based on cost,
the presumption is that inventories will also be stated at cost.

2. *Definition of cost.* Cost of inventories is acquisition and production cost. It is the price paid or consideration given upon acquisition.

3. *Write-down as revised cost.* If inventories have been written

down below cost, the reduced book figure is accounted for as cost in the subsequent accounting period.

4. *Cost inclusions.* Cost includes all direct and indirect expenditures and charges incurred to bring merchandise to its existing condition and location so that it may be used for its intended purpose.

5. *Allocation problems.* Difficult problems arise in the allocation of costs, particularly to work in process and finished goods. Sometimes, charges such as idle facility expense, excessive spoilage, double freight, and rehandling costs are so abnormal that they should not be capitalized to inventories, but should, on the contrary, be expensed as period costs.

6. *General and administrative expenses.* If such expenses are clearly related to production, the allocable amount may be included in inventory cost; otherwise, they should be expensed as period costs.

7. *Selling expenses.* These expenses are not includable in the cost of inventories.

8. *Overhead.* It is not acceptable to exclude all overhead from inventory costs.

9. *Cost accounting system.* Any cost accounting system must be individually evaluated as to adequacy of procedures, soundness of principles, and consistency.

Flow of Cost

1. *Assumptions as to flow.* Inventory costs may be determined by any one of several assumptions as to flow of costs.

2. *Objective.* The objective in selection of the costing method is the clear reflection of periodic income.

3. *Specifically identified cost.* In some businesses, inventory items are individually identified from time of purchase to time of sale and are costed on the basis of specifically identified cost.

4. *Fifo, Lifo, Average.* If purchases of substantially identical and interchangeable merchandise are made at different times, the use of specifically identified cost may not produce the most useful financial statements, even if the identity of the goods is not lost between purchase and sale. Additional practical and acceptable bases for costing are Fifo (first-in, first-out), Lifo (last-in, first-out), and Average.

5. *Retail method.* In some situations, a reversed mark-up procedure of pricing, like the retail inventory method, may be practical and appropriate.

6. *Standard costs.* Such costs are acceptable if they are adjusted periodically so that as of the balance sheet date they approximate

one of the acceptable pricing methods. Proper statement presentation should utilize appropriate phraseology such as "standard costs, approximating average costs" or "approximate costs determined on a first-in, first-out basis."

7. *Use of several methods.* Depending on the nature of business operations, one acceptable method may be used for one type of inventory and other acceptable methods may be applied to other portions.

8. *Uniform industry practice.* Financial statements would be more useful if all companies within an industry were to adopt uniform methods of inventory pricing.

Loss of Utility

1. *Cost and utility.* Cost is the proper basis of accounting for inventories if there has been no decline in the utility of the goods subsequent to acquisition.

2. *Decline in utility.* A loss should be recognized in the current period when the utility of goods, as viewed in terms of disposal in the ordinary course of business, is less than cost.

3. *Reasons for decline.* A decline in utility of goods may occur as a result of damage, deterioration, changes in price levels, or other factors.

4. *Market.* When a loss is recognized, the lower amount at which inventories are stated is referred to as market.

5. *Lower of cost or market.* Stating the inventories at cost or market, whichever is lower, reflects a practical rule for measuring the remaining utility inherent in the inventories and for determining the recognized loss.

6. *Presentation of loss.* When substantial and unusual losses are recorded in applying the rule of lower of cost or market, it is desirable to disclose the loss in the income statement separately from cost of goods sold.

Meaning of Market

1. *Current utility.* Market is the measure of the current utility of the inventories at the balance sheet date.

2. *Current expenditure.* Market may therefore be viewed as representing the current expenditure that would have to be made at the statement date in order to obtain inventories having equivalent current usefulness.

3. *Replacement market.* As a general rule, therefore, market is the current replacement market, that is, the current cost of purchasing or manufacturing the merchandise.

4. *Upper limit-net realizable value.* But market should not be higher than the net realizable value. Net realizable value is the estimated selling price less reasonably determinable costs of completion and disposal. Replacement market would not properly measure the utility of the inventories if the net realizable amount upon sale is lower than the replacement or reproduction cost.

5. *Lower limit-net realizable value reduced by an approximately normal profit margin.* Market should not be lower than the net realizable value reduced by a normal profit margin. If inventories can be sold at a price to permit recovery of cost and also to realize a normal profit, it would be improper to show a loss even though replacement market is lower than this lower limit. The salability of the merchandise at a normal profit may be evidenced by the holding of firm sales contracts at fixed prices or having a sufficient volume of future orders at stable selling prices.

6. *Guide versus fixed rule.* The foregoing is to be regarded as a guide rather than a fixed rule in the determination of market and market declines.

(a) *Retail inventory method.* Thus, if adequate markdowns are recorded, the retail inventory method will also reflect the rule of lower cost or market.

(b) *Future losses.* Also, inventories should not be written down simply to reduce or eliminate losses that are an inherent part of future operations. This cautionary note is especially applicable if the business is expected to incur losses for a sustained period.

(c) *Temporary fluctuations.* Moreover, selling prices may not be affected by small or temporary fluctuations in replacement or reproduction costs.

Lower of Cost or Market-Applications of Rule

1. *Item-by-item.* The most common practice is to apply the rule of lower cost or market on an item-by-item basis.

2. *Total inventory.* If there is only one end product, however, periodic income would be more fairly stated if cost and market were arrived at for the inventories as a whole and the lower of total cost or total market were selected in applying the rule.

3. *Inventory categories.* When there is more than one major product or category, the rule may be applied to the totals of such categories. The use of totals rather than the item-by-item method is especially indicated when the market of some components is below cost while the market of others in the same general categories of finished goods is higher than cost, so that no overall loss results. But

if an effective method of classifying inventories by categories is not adopted, the item-by-item method should be employed.

4. *Balanced quantities.* When it is proper to apply the rule to totals rather than to individual items, care must be exercised to determine that the items are in balanced quantities. When certain items are in excess quantity in relation to other components, the lower of cost or market rule is applied to the excess quantities on an item-by-item basis. The individual item method also applies if such items are used in the production of unrelated products or of products whose turnover rate varies materially.

Basis of Stating Inventories-Disclosure and Consistency

1. *Disclosure.* The basis of stating inventories and method of costing should be disclosed in the financial statements.

2. *Consistency.* Inventories should be stated on a consistent basis so that periodic income may be fairly reported and allocated between years.

3. *Change in method.* If there has been a change in the method of stating inventories, there should be a full disclosure of the nature of the change and of its effect upon income.

Stating Inventories above Cost

1. *Accrual of income.* Income accrues only at the time of sale; gains may not be anticipated by recording assets at selling prices. Only in exceptional cases may inventories be stated above cost.

2. *Precious metals.* An exception to the above cost rule exists for gold and silver which are ordinarily stated at selling prices when there is a government-controlled market at a fixed monetary value and the costs of marketing therefore are not substantial.

3. *Other inventories.* A similar exception applies to inventories of agricultural, minerals, and other products which have interchangeable units with immediate marketability at quoted prices and whose costs are difficult to obtain.

4. *Presentation.* When such inventories are stated at selling prices, they should be reduced by subsequent disposal costs and the basis of valuation should be disclosed in the financial statements.

Losses on Purchase Commitments

1. *Recognition of loss.* Losses from uncancelable and unhedged purchase commitments should be recognized and measured in the same way as inventory losses.

2. *Nonrecognition.* No loss on purchase commitments occurs if

there are firm offsetting sales contracts or other assurances of continuing sales without price decline.

3. *Disclosure.* Material losses on purchase commitments should be separately disclosed in the income statement.

COST ACCOUNTING CONCEPTS

Cost accounting is designed to measure the costs of products, manufacturing processes, and the operations of departments, divisions, and other component segments of the entity, whereas financial accounting is concerned with aggregate costs for income determination with respect to the entity as a whole.

In conjunction with its more common application to inventory cost determination, cost accounting is employed to provide management with a variety of methods of analysis for planning, controlling, and evaluating the performance of the enterprise and its segments.

Cost accounting may sometimes draw upon concepts which differ from those which are compatible with generally accepted accounting principles. The use of such concepts is entirely appropriate for internal accounting purposes, but where they are reflected in the general books of account these books must later be adjusted so that the financial statements for general reporting purposes are in conformity with generally accepted accounting principles. The following are some of the commonly used cost accounting concepts.

1. *Standard versus actual costs.* Standard costs are predetermined costs of manufacturing and represent standards of operating efficiency. Differences between standard costs and actual costs are referred to as variances and are useful in measuring the efficiency of the manufacturing effort.

2. *Direct versus indirect costs.* Direct costs are those costs which can, with reasonable effort, be identified with or traced to the specific products or segments under study. In contrast, indirect costs like manufacturing overhead expenses are those which cannot be so identified and must therefore be allocated to products on some rational basis.

3. *Allocation of manufacturing overhead.* Manufacturing overhead consists of indirect material, indirect labor, and plant manufacturing expenses. The allocation basis used to apply aggregate overhead costs to units of production will be considered adequate to the extent that it measures reliably the proportionate amount of overhead incurred

in manufacturing the different products. Commonly used bases of allocation are: unit; direct material cost; direct labor cost; direct labor hours; prime cost; and machine hours. The suitability of the different bases will vary with the nature of the manufacturing operation. For example, the unit basis would be appropriate where a limited variety of products is manufactured requiring essentially the same amount of material, labor, and processing operations. Where labor is the principal cost in the production process, labor hours or cost provides a useful basis. In a highly automated operation, machine hours would be appropriate.

4. *Overhead rates.* Overhead rates (the ratio of total overhead costs to total volume of production expressed in terms of labor hours, machine hours, or other basis of allocation) may be determined in advance of the period to which they apply. They are then referred to as predetermined overhead rates in contrast to historical rates based on actual costs and production. The former is the more common approach because it avoids the distortion of short-run influences by assuming a normal level of production, and also facilitates costing on a current basis.

5. *Fixed versus variable costs.* Fixed costs, such as rent and depreciation, are referred to as such because, within given ranges of output, they do not vary with changes in the volume of production. On the other hand, variable costs do vary with volume. This distinction is important in arriving at break-even points and in measuring the impact of changes in sales volume on costs and profits.

6. *Controllable versus noncontrollable cost.* Costs may also be differentiated in accordance with whether they are controllable at the given level of management. The idea here is to tie in the costs with the personnel responsible for their incurrence and utilization.

7. *Out-of-pocket costs.* Out-of-pocket costs require the current outlay of funds and may be contrasted with book costs, such as depreciation, representing expenditures already made. This distinction is important in decisions of alternative choice such as make-or-buy in which the amount of additional out-of-pocket costs becomes a significant factor.

8. *Incremental costs.* Incremental costs are the additional costs that would be incurred as a result of increases in plant capacity or other changes in the nature or scope of operations. This concept is applied in computing the additional cost that would be incurred, and incremental costs are often distinguished from sunk costs such as investment in plant and equipment that would not be altered as a result of the decision.

9. *Opportunity (or imputed) costs.* The profit which might have resulted from an alternative use of limited facilities is referred to as opportunity or imputed cost. The profit foregone is thus viewed as a sacrifice or cost to be considered in arriving at the cost of the facilities committed to the particular project.

10. *Joint costs.* Also referred to as common costs, joint costs are not identifiable with or traceable to a specific product or process. It then becomes necessary to arrive at a proper basis for allocating the joint costs to the several products to which they relate.

11. *Byproducts.* A byproduct is a type of joint product, but may require little or no processing after the point of split-off from the major product. Since the manufacture of byproducts is quite incidental to the manufacture of the major products, practices vary with respect to the assignment of costs to the byproduct; some companies for example assign no cost to byproducts while others may allocate only byproduct costs incurred after the split-off.

FIXED ASSETS AND DEPRECIATION

The accounting research bulletins touch only upon special aspects of the accounting for fixed assets and depreciation as in ARB No. 43, Chapter 9, which deals with depreciation with respect to high costs, appreciation, and emergency facilities, and ARB No. 44 (revised) which is concerned with declining-balance depreciation. The following is a summary of the broad major principles governing the accounting for fixed assets and depreciation.

1. *Cost.* Fixed assets should be stated at cost.

2. *Elements of cost.* Cost includes all expenditures necessary to acquire or construct the asset and to locate it and put it in a condition suitable and operable for the intended use. The following are some typical elements of cost: invoice price less trade and cash discounts; legal expenses related to acquisition as well as title search and insurance fees and brokerage commissions; freight and delivery, installation and testing; demolition costs on buildings acquired for land sites; overhead allocable to construction.

3. *Noncash acquisitions.* If fixed assets are acquired in exchange for capital stock or for noncash assets, the cost of the assets acquired is the fair value of the assets received or the fair value of the consideration given, whichever is the more clearly evident. Basically, the cost of an asset is measured by the value of the asset given

up in exchange—usually cash or an obligation to pay cash—but it is presumed that the asset acquired will have a value corresponding to its cash cost and confirmed in an objective exchange entered into on an arms-length basis and characterized by rationality. The par or stated value of stock given in exchange is not in itself indicative of value.

4. *Capital versus expense.* Repair and replacement expenditures which prolong the life of a fixed asset or enhance its operating efficiency materially beyond that expected from normal repair and maintenance, may be properly capitalized.

5. *Depreciation—allocation versus valuation.* Fixed assets should be depreciated over their economically useful lives. As a process of allocation and not of valuation, depreciation is designed to achieve a proper matching of cost and revenue rather than a balance sheet valuation suggestive of resale or realizable values. The focus is on fair income determination.

6. *Systematic and rational method.* Depreciation must be recorded on a systematic and rational basis to preclude the possibility of arbitrary write-offs or of charges to income which could result in equalizing or otherwise manipulating income from one period to the next.

7. *Consistency.* Depreciation methods should be consistently applied from period to period. If there is any change in method, the fact of the change must be disclosed as well as the effect of the change on income and balance sheet.

8. *Matching of cost and revenue.* The purpose of depreciation is to match cost with related revenue. The units-of-production method most clearly reflects this direct relationship, whereas other methods seek to accomplish the same objective by apportioning costs to periods of time.

9. *Useful life—estimate and judgment.* Determining the useful life of a fixed asset is a matter of estimate and judgment because of the element of uncertainty.

10. *Uncertainty.* The element of uncertainty may exist with respect to: obsolescence; physical life; future scrap value; future revenue and relative amounts of revenue in early and later years; maintenance policy; price-level; future replacement cost.

11. *Physical versus economic utility.* To be emphasized is the principle that depreciation is concerned with the economic utility of the fixed asset and not with the physical life *per se.*

12. *Conservatism.* Because of the factors which make for uncertainty, the accelerated depreciation methods (declining-balance or

sum-of-years-digits) may be favored by some accountants on the ground of conservatism. But it should be recognized that, as compared with straight-line depreciation for example, the accelerated methods are less conservative in later years.

13. *Practicality.* Some depreciation methods may be selected because they are more practical in terms of cost and recordkeeping—the straight-line, for example, in preference to the machine-hours or units-of-production.

14. *Income taxes.* The method chosen for income tax purposes may differ from that chosen for the financial statements. It is the latter which must reflect generally accepted accounting principles. Hence, shorter lives permitted for emergency facilities with respect to taxes need not necessarily be used for accounting purposes. Moreover, tax allocation principles must be followed where the tax and book depreciation methods differ.

15. *Depreciation on appreciation.* When fixed assets are written up to appreciated values or to any amount above cost (less accumulated depreciation), depreciation must be recorded on the appreciation. The balance sheet representation of increased values creates an obligation to depreciate the increased asset amount in the same manner as the regular asset.

16. *Appreciation of fixed assets.* In general, however, and except mainly for quasi-reorganizations, it is improper to write up fixed assets or to state them on any basis except cost less accumulated depreciation.

17. *Depreciation and high costs.* See discussion on page 151.

18. *Depreciation rate adjustments.* If it is later determined that the useful life of the asset is longer or shorter than originally estimated, an adjustment in depreciation rate can properly be made so that the undepreciated balance would be written off over the remaining useful life. However, if a materially shortened life would necessitate such substantial depreciation charges as to make the income statements misleading, a partial write-down may be made to retained earnings.

19. *Source of funds.* Depreciation is a process of allocation of costs (fixed assets) to income and yet it is sometimes referred to as being a source of funds. This concept probably originates because depreciation is one of the noncash charges added to the figure of net income in preparing the statement of source and application of funds. (The reader may wish to read at this point the discussion on that subject in Chapter 5.) Depreciation charges by themselves,

however, as recorded in the accounts do not represent sources of funds, although revenues received may be viewed as consisting of a recovery of costs (including depreciation) plus profit.

PREPAID EXPENSES, DEFERRED CHARGES, AND INTANGIBLE ASSETS

Prepaid expenses, deferred charges, and intangibles are separately classified on the balance sheet but they are often considered as a unit because of the following features which they have in common:

1. They are acquired by purchase or outlays (or the equivalent, where acquired in exchange for capital stock).

2. The justification for recording them as assets is that their utility extends beyond the balance sheet date.

3. They are unexpired costs and their utility consists in their applicability to future operations rather than in any recoveries from resale or liquidation.

4. They are written off to operations over the period to be benefited on a reasonable and consistent basis.

5. Any diminution in utility either in whole or in part, aside from the decline represented by the periodic write-off, must be immediately reflected in a corresponding write-off of the asset balance.

6. Any established change in the period of utility, as originally estimated, would require a change in the amortization rate.

It should be helpful, preliminary to a further discussion of these assets, to list several examples of each type.

1. *Prepaid expenses.* Prepaid (unexpired) insurance, prepaid interest, prepaid rent, prepaid taxes, prepaid advertising, unused office supplies, expense advances.

2. *Deferred charges.* Research and development costs, organization expense (frequently classified under intangibles), leasehold, plant rearrangement costs, unamortized bond discount.

3. *Intangibles.* Patents, copyrights, franchises, goodwill, trade names and trademarks, organization expense, formulas and processes.

INTANGIBLES—INITIAL CARRYING VALUE

Intangibles are assets which provide or reflect a special and sometimes exclusive privilege or advantage, frequently of a monopolistic character. Accounting Research Bulletin No. 43, Chapter 5, is a rather comprehensive statement on the problems involved in accounting for intangibles. A summary of this chapter together with our interpretive comments are provided in this and the succeeding sections.

1. *Cost.* Intangibles should be stated at cost.

2. *Full-cost.* Cost should include all expenditures made for the acquisition or construction of the asset and for placing it in a condition suitable for use. Thus, legal fees, state filing fees, and similar expenses are capitalized as intangibles where relevant to the asset's acquisition.

3. *Noncash acquisitions.* If intangibles are acquired in exchange for capital stock or for noncash assets, the cost of the intangibles is the fair value of the intangibles received or the fair value of the consideration given, whichever is the more clearly evident.

4. *Basket purchase.* If a number of intangibles or a combination of tangible and intangible property are acquired for a lump-sum consideration in a basket purchase, an appropriate allocation of the aggregate cost should be made to the specific assets acquired. Such allocation is necessary so that the individual assets may be amortized on the basis of their individual cost and useful lives. An accountability is also thereby created for the subsequent determination of gain or loss upon disposition.

5. *Investment in subsidiary.* In the event that the cost to the parent company of the investment in a purchased subsidiary is greater than the parent's equity in the subsidiary's assets at the acquisition date as reflected on the subsidiary's books, then the excess must be accounted for in accordance with its true nature. If any part of the excess is attributable to intangible assets or to the general goodwill of the subsidiary, appropriate amounts should be allocated to these or other assets involved.

AMORTIZATION OF INTANGIBLES

Inasmuch as the utility of intangibles and their economic value to the enterprise are often somewhat removed from the realization of revenue, the determination of useful life and of periodic amortization presents considerable difficulties. The major principles applicable to the amortization and write-down of intangibles are stated in ARB No. 43, Chapter 5.

Question—May 1962 (6)

The amortization and write-down or write-off of intangible assets involve basic accounting principles of balance sheet presentation and income determination.

(a) Give the two broad classifications or types of intangible assets and indicate the factors you would consider in classifying them.

(b) State the generally accepted accounting procedures for the amortization, write-down or write-off of the two classifications of intangible assets.

(c) It has been argued, on the grounds of conservatism, that all intangible assets should be written off immediately after acquisition. Give the accounting arguments against this treatment.

Solution

Classification

Intangibles may be broadly classified into two categories.

1. *Limited life.* Those which have a limited useful life and would be amortized on that basis. The limited life may be determined by law. Thus, patents have a 17-year legal life and copyrights 28 years with renewal privilege for another 28 years. In other cases, such as franchises, licenses, and leases, the limited life may be determined by agreement. In still other instances, the limited term of existence may result from the very nature of the intangible such as a manufacturing process subject to obsolescence.

2. *Unlimited life.* Those which have no such limited term of existence and may be said to have either an unlimited life, an indefinite life, or one in which there is no evidence of limited duration. Some examples of these are goodwill, going value, trade names, perpetual franchises, and organization costs. The characterization of an intangible as having an unlimited life would be made at acquisition although a review of its status in that regard would have to be made periodically thereafter.

Principles of Amortization—Limited-Life Intangibles

1. *Useful life.* Intangibles which have a limited life should be amortized over that period.

2. *Benefit.* The period of useful life should be the same as the period during which the enterprise will be benefited by the intangible.

3. *Utility and legal factor.* By the utility of the intangible we mean

its economic utility. Consequently the period of useful life can often be less than the legal life and, more rarely, longer. Similarly, the useful life can be less than that based on a lease or other agreement.

4. *Systematic amortization.* Amortization must be recorded on a systematic and rational basis in order to avoid arbitrary charges from period to period and the improper shifting of income.

5. *Change in period.* If the period benefited is determined later to be longer or shorter than originally estimated, this fact should be recognized by: (a) change in rate of amortization to reflect the changed life; (b) but, if increased charges to income are thereby necessitated which would distort the income of future years, a partial write-down may be made to retained earnings so that the subsequent charges to income may be reduced.

6. *Loss of utility.* Even apart from a reduction in original estimated life, an intangible may suffer a recognizable loss in original utility. In that event, as in the case of all losses, the impairment must be recognized by an immediate write-down corresponding to the amount of the loss. If the entire asset becomes worthless, the full cost should be immediately written off. The write-down should be made to retained earnings if the charge to income would be so material as to make the income statement misleading.

Principles of Amortization—Unlimited-Life Intangibles

1. *No amortization.* Intangibles which have an indefinite useful life may be retained on the books without amortization so long as the utility remains unimpaired and the term of existence continues to be indefinite.

2. *Systematic amortization.* Unlimited-term intangibles may, alternatively, be amortized periodically in accordance with the following principles:

(a) *Corporate decision.* The decision to amortize may be made either as a simple matter of accounting policy or when the corporation decides that, despite original expectations, the intangible may not continue to have value during the entire life of the company. This decision can be made even where there is no present indication of limited existence or diminution in utility and even though expenditures are being made to maintain the asset's value.

(b) *Reasonableness.* The plan of amortization must be systematic and reasonable and based on all relevant circumstances. Thus, if the intangible is closely related to the production of revenue and its utility is being maintained, the period of amortization can be relatively long.

(c) *Justification for amortization.* The justification for amortization of unlimited-life intangibles largely rests on the grounds of uncertainty, that is, uncertainty as to whether an asset can have an eternal life and uncertainty with respect to measurement of the asset's remaining utility. Also to be considered is the desirability of each year's income statement bearing an appropriate periodic charge, a procedure which would not be possible in the absence of systematic amortization.

3. *Change to limited life.* If it becomes evident that the life of the intangible has become limited, the amortization principles followed for limited-term intangibles would then apply. Specifically, the cost should be amortized over the estimated remaining life. But if the remaining period is so short that the ensuing periodic charges to income would be so material as to make the income statements misleading, a partial write-down may be made to retained earnings, and the balance of the cost would then be amortized over the remaining useful life.

4. *Loss of utility.* The principles regarding the loss of utility for limited-term intangibles similarly apply to those having an indefinite term of existence.

Write-Off upon Acquisition

1. *Impropriety.* It is improper to make a lump-sum write-off of intangibles immediately after acquisition.

2. *Worthless asset.* The foregoing rule assumes, of course, that there has been no impairment in the expected utility of the asset. But if a loss did so materialize immediately after acquisition, the loss would have to be recognized.

3. *Capital surplus versus retained earnings.* ARB No. 43, Chapter 5, indicates that any such lump-sum write-off should never be made to capital surplus. Any write-off pertaining to operations would naturally be charged to income and, if material and extraordinary, to retained earnings. A charge to capital surplus could only be recorded if capital surplus had been credited upon the acquisition of the asset, and the write-off represented in effect an adjustment of the original capital stock transaction.

4. *Conservatism.* The principle of conservatism does not state that assets should be reduced or eliminated where they continue to exist. Moreover, it is improper to write off an asset in its entirety in one period simply because of difficulties in estimating the useful life. A systematic plan of amortization conforms with the idea of conservatism.

5. *Income determination.* The write-off immediately upon acquisition would preclude the future periodic charges to income and thus distort the income of future years.

6. *Balance sheet misrepresentation.* The elimination of the asset would improperly remove from the balance sheet an asset which will yield future benefits.

GOODWILL

Goodwill is an intangible asset whose utility is usually regarded as consisting of the value placed upon the excess earning capacity of an enterprise. The accounting principles governing the recording of goodwill and its amortization are the same as those which apply to intangibles generally.

Question—May 1959 (4a,b)

Goodwill which is permitted on a statement (other than a consolidated statement) is that which has been purchased. Describe briefly two explanations which have been used to justify the recording of goodwill in the balance sheet of a corporation or partnership.

Present two methods for estimating the value of goodwill in determining the amount which should properly be paid for it.

Solution

1. *Cost.* As in the case of other assets, goodwill is recorded on the books only when purchased, and at cost.

2. *Asset value.* Goodwill is an intangible asset and, having value as an asset, is properly recorded on the balance sheet. However, goodwill may be the single term used to cover a variety of circumstances which, if properly analyzed, would disclose variations in utility and, possibly, in useful life depending upon the particular circumstances. Several of the more common ways in which goodwill may be interpreted (to which methods of estimating its value may correspond) are listed in the remainder of this section.

3. *Excess profits.* Goodwill may represent the amount paid for the capacity of an enterprise to earn a rate of annual profits in excess of the average rate earned in the industry. In computing its value in this manner, any of the following methods might be used: (a) capitalization of average excess profits on the basis of the normal

profit percentage, or even by the use of some arbitrary rate; (b) average excess profits multiplied by a certain number of years; (c) the present value of an annuity corresponding to the excess profits for a given number of years.

4. *Consolidated goodwill.* Goodwill may arise as the excess of the purchase price of the subsidiary's capital stock over the book value of the parent company's share of the subsidiary's net assets as shown on the latter's books as of the date of acquisition. This amount may or may not represent goodwill and should be assigned, where applicable, to specific tangible and intangible assets. In some instances where the excess amount so paid cannot be assigned to particular assets and, in addition, is something other than goodwill, it should be designated on the balance sheet by an appropriate title to signify its origin.

5. *Going concern.* The amount paid for goodwill may represent the value of the going concern above the aggregate value assignable to specific assets purchased.

6. *Special benefits.* The extra amount paid supposedly for goodwill may actually represent an amount paid for special benefits such as subscription lists, customer lists, a working organization, competence of personnel, technological expertness, etc. In some instances it may consist of the amount of earnings for the first few years of the going organization in excess of the earnings for the same period for a newly formed organization.

AMORTIZATION OF GOODWILL

The essential principles that relate to the amortization of goodwill correspond to those previously set forth for intangible assets, particularly for unlimited-life intangibles.

Question—November 1959 (5d)

How, if at all, should goodwill, properly recorded on the books, be amortized in order to conform with generally accepted accounting principles?

Solution

1. *Amortization of intangibles.* Goodwill should be amortized over its useful life in the same manner as other intangibles.

2. *Knowledge at date of acquisition.* The more explicit the knowledge at the date of acquisition regarding the nature of the asset acquired, the more enlightened will be the plan of amortization. Thus, if the amount paid represents the expected excess earnings for a limited number of years, goodwill can be amortized over that period.

3. *Indefinite life.* If it is expected that the asset will have a value for an indefinite period, or eternally, the asset may be retained on the books without amortization or, alternatively, amortized over a reasonable period in accordance with a systematic and rational plan.

The reader may wish to review the earlier discussion on the amortization of intangibles in general because many of those ideas are specifically applicable to goodwill and its write-off.

PREPAID EXPENSES AND DEFERRED CHARGES

With few exceptions, prepaid expenses and deferred charges may almost be regarded as intangible assets in the sense that their value does not depend on physical property. However, as we have stated, assets usually classified as intangibles are those which are possessed of a special and sometimes monopolistic privilege. Prepaid expenses and deferred charges are often distinguished mainly on the basis of time, the former being classified as current assets and the latter as long-term.

Question—November 1955 (7c)

Explain the nature of deferred charges, including the final disposition of them, and the distinction between deferred charges and prepaid expenses.

Solution

The distinction between the two accounts will be drawn by way of a separate listing of the characteristics of each.

Prepaid Expenses

1. Prepaid expenses are assets which represent services or benefits paid for or accrued as of the balance sheet date, which have not been consumed, utilized, or received as of this date.

2. The asset will be written off to expense subsequent to the balance

sheet date and over the period of their consumption, service, or benefit to be received.

3. Because the period of write-off is usually within a year after the balance sheet date (or, if longer than a year, within the normal operating cycle for the business), prepaid expenses (unlike deferred charges or intangibles) are classified as current assets. An additional justification for classifying prepaid expenses as current is that, if they had not been paid for or recorded in advance of their utilization, they would have required the use of working capital during the subsequent period.

4. Prepaid expenses usually relate to normal recurring business expenses.

5. In many instances these assets would have a realizable value upon liquidation although the assets are recorded and amortized on a going-concern basis.

6. The period of useful life is usually clearly determinable by reference to the agreement with the outside party: for example, the lease, insurance policy, or borrowing arrangement.

Deferred Charges

1. Deferred charges are assets which represent expenditures made as of the balance sheet date having a utility or value in subsequent accounting periods.

2. The asset will be charged-off to operations over the periods to which the benefits are applicable.

3. Since the period to be benefited usually is long-term and extends beyond a year (or operating cycle) subsequent to the balance sheet date, these assets are noncurrent.

4. They may be further distinguished from prepaid expenses in that:

(a) Deferred charges do not (as contrasted with certain prepaid expenses) involve payments to outside parties in advance of services to be received from these parties.

(b) Their period of utility is frequently indeterminable and, therefore, is sometimes arbitrarily determined.

(c) Sudden losses in value may require lump-sum write-offs, in whole or in part, as nonoperating deductions or as charges to retained earnings if so material as to make the income statement misleading.

5. They have a going-concern value rather than a liquidation value.

6. On the ground of conservatism and in view of the uncertainty regarding the period of useful life, companies may either amortize deferred charges over a shorter period than ordinarily warranted or

follow a consistent policy of expensing deferred charges in full in the initial year.

RESEARCH AND DEVELOPMENT COSTS

The following discussion will help to pinpoint the uncertainties which surround a representative deferred charge such as research and development costs.

1. *Success.* It is frequently difficult to estimate with any reasonable degree of assurance the future success of such undertakings.

2. *Single versus multiple projects.* The risk of misstatement with respect to both capitalization and amortization is greater if we are dealing with a single research project as compared to a variety. If a single project is unsuccessful, the impact is far greater than if only one or a few of many projects turn out to be unsuccessful.

3. *Type of project.* The very type of project may affect the degree of uncertainty. Thus research costs pertaining to a new product would suggest stronger grounds for conservatism than those relating to proven products. Similar distinctions might be made depending upon whether the costs pertain to manufacturing, marketing, processes, products, etc.

4. *Recurring versus special.* In the case of recurring projects even such an extreme policy as the full write-off of costs would have little effect on the income statement if consistently applied. Such a policy, however, for special projects would severely affect the comparability of income statements from year to year.

5. *Assignment of costs.* It is sometimes difficult to assign certain overhead costs to particular research projects. This may necessitate in some instances the treatment of all research projects as a unit, and in others the lump-sum write-off of costs to the current period.

6. *Continuous research.* In industries where continuous research is a necessary part of the regular operations of the business, research costs may be viewed as period costs to be charged to income in full as incurred.

CAPITALIZATION OF "LOSSES"

Representing as they do expenditures which provide no benefit for the enterprise, losses by their very nature cannot be deferred as assets and must be written off immediately. However, in the case particularly of a new business or a new operation, normal preoperating expenditures may be properly capitalized.

Question—November 1955 (7b)

Discuss the treatment of losses that occur in a new business prior to realization of any operational revenue.

Solution

1. *Absence of retained earnings.* It may be argued that these losses should be deferred as assets to be written off against income of future periods, on the ground that there is no balance of retained earnings against which to charge the losses. This argument is invalid because losses cannot be deferred and can be charged to a deficit account in the absence of retained earnings.

2. *Absence of revenue.* Losses are not expenses or costs to be matched with revenue, but rather are to be written off immediately as period costs.

3. *Analysis of loss.* What was initially considered a loss may, after appropriate analysis, be recognized as representing a combination of elements—assets, expenses, and perhaps losses, as noted in the following.

4. *Organization expense.* Some of the charges previously considered to be losses may represent expenditures for the organization of the company which can therefore be capitalized as organization expenses.

5. *Deferred charges or other assets.* Similarly, certain of the expenditures may represent either fixed assets to be capitalized as such or deferred charges representing perhaps initial research and development expenses which will have a utility for future periods.

6. *Initial loss as necessity.* The position may be taken that in the initial period of the life of an enterprise or in the early stages of a new business operation, it is customary to experience losses; until the enterprise has reached its expected level of operations, out of necessity such "losses" will be incurred. It can then be concluded that expenditures which are so necessary in the subsequent achievement of revenue should be regarded as assets—deferred charges to be initially capitalized as such for subsequent write-off against revenue.

7. *Uncertainty and conservatism.* A significant response to the preceding argument is that there is uncertainty, particularly for a new enterprise, regarding the realization of future revenue; thus conservatism dictates that the losses be recognized as such and not capitalized as deferred charges.

8. *Capital deduction.* An initial loss may sometimes represent an adjustment of the original accounting entry recording the contribution of capital by stockholders. An example of this might be a possible overvaluation of assets contributed to the corporation in exchange for capital stock. A write-down of such assets in the form of an adjustment to the original valuation would constitute a deduction from contributed capital rather than an operating loss.

CHAPTER 4

REPORTING PRINCIPLES AND STANDARDS

The entire framework of accounting concepts which comprise the generally accepted accounting principles constitutes in effect the reporting principles and standards designed to achieve fairness in financial reporting. In this chapter we will be concerned specifically with technical reporting principles and standards relating to informative disclosure, comparability and consistency, contingencies and conditions of uncertainty.

THE STANDARD OF INFORMATIVE DISCLOSURE

The concept of informative disclosure which was introduced in Chapter 1 can also be looked upon as a standard of reporting affecting the responsibilities of both management and the independent accountant.

The fairness of the financial statements encompasses not only their conformity with generally accepted accounting principles, but also the matter of informative disclosures. While it is difficult to separate the two features because they are so closely allied, the difference becomes more distinct if it is recognized that financial statements may technically conform with accepted principles and yet fail to reflect adequate disclosure of material matters whose disclosure is necessary to make the statements not misleading.

It is the primary and fundamental responsibility of management to provide the necessary disclosures in proper form in the financial statements (which, it is to be understood, also include the related notes). But when the client declines to do so, the auditor is obliged by the third reporting standard of the generally accepted auditing standards to disclose the data in his certificate and to appropriately qualify his opinion. The reporting standard reads as follows:

"Informative disclosures in the financial statements are to be regarded as reasonably adequate unless otherwise stated in the report."

The area covered by this standard is often referred to as *statement presentation* because it is essentially concerned with the adequacy in presentation of the form and content of the statements and their appended notes.

DISCLOSURE OF DEPARTURES FROM APB OPINIONS

A special bulletin issued by the AICPA in 1964, entitled "Disclosure of Departures From Opinions of Accounting Principles Board," sets forth the recommendations adopted by the AICPA's Council to the effect that auditors are required to see that disclosures are made either in footnotes to financial statements or in their audit reports regarding departures from APB *Opinions*. The following is a summary of this bulletin.

1. *Accounting principles.* Generally accepted accounting principles are defined as those which have substantial authoritative support.
2. *Authoritative support.* While APB Opinions do constitute "substantial authoritative support," authoritative support can exist for principles that differ from the Opinions.
3. *Effect of departure from APB Opinions.* If a company has used an accounting principle that varies materially in its effect from one accepted in an APB Opinion, the auditor must act as follows:

(a) *Evaluation of principle.* He must decide whether there is substantial authoritative support for the principle adopted and whether it is applicable in the circumstances of the individual company.

(b) *Existence of support.* If such support does exist, then the auditor could render an unqualified opinion; but he must see to it that the departure is disclosed either in a footnote to the financial statements or in a separate paragraph in the auditor's report.

(c) *Form of disclosure.* If practical, the effect of the departure on the financial statements should likewise be disclosed, but if the approximate effect on the statements cannot be reasonably determined, that fact should be explicitly noted. Since an unqualified opinion is being rendered, in order to avoid confusion it would be desirable, after a recitation of the facts of the departure and its effects, to note that the company's treatment has substantial authoritative support and is an acceptable practice.

(d) *Absence of support.* If the auditor decides that there is an absence of substantial support for a material departure from an APB Opinion, he would qualify his opinion, disclaim an opinion, or submit an adverse opinion, depending upon the circumstances.

4. *Substandard reporting.* The failure to disclose material departures, as indicated, is to be judged as substandard reporting.

GENERAL AREAS AND TYPES OF DISCLOSURES

The following is a listing of some important general areas and types of informative disclosures which conform with current reporting theory and practice.

1. *Classification.* The classification of items on the financial statements must be such as to present meaningfully and logically the financial condition of the company and the results of its operations. Appropriate cognizance must be taken of the need to reveal similarities, dissimilarities, and relationships. Illustrative of these principles are: the use of captions and total figures to designate the aggregate of subordinate groupings such as inventories or major divisions such as assets and capital; clear differentiation between current and noncurrent assets and liabilities; the grouping of expenses by operating function, such as cost of sales, selling, and administrative; and the clear showing of deductions such as sales returns and valuation allowance accounts from related gross amounts.

2. *Terminology.* Unclear and unprecise terminology may be confusing to the reader. For example, the use of the term *reserve* is now restricted to surplus reserves. Its former additional use in conjunction with valuation allowances and estimated liabilities was bewildering to the reader because the term not only erroneously conveyed the idea of reserve amounts being set aside, but was also used as a single label to cover essentially *different* types of accounts.

3. *Accounting principles followed.* The bases of valuation of certain assets are customarily disclosed; for example, that fixed assets are stated at cost.

4. *Accounting method employed.* Sometimes, such as for inventories, both the accounting principle and the accounting method are noted. A typical comment as to inventories might read: "At the lower of first-in first-out cost or market."

5. *Market value.* Although investments are stated at cost, it is customary to disclose parenthetically their current market value. This rule, however, is only selectively applied; for example, market values of inventories are not so disclosed.

6. *Changes in accounting principles.* Inconsistencies in the application of accounting principles or changes in accounting methods as between years, must be disclosed, along with the effect of such changes on the income statement and balance sheet.

7. *Comparability.* Apart from changes in accounting methods, significant changes in the operations of a company may affect the comparability of financial statements. Appropriate disclosure of such events and their effect on comparability can help to avoid the drawing of misleading inferences.

8. *Conditions, restrictions, and obligations.* The nature of any material conditions, restrictions, or obligations surrounding assets, liabilities, and capital should be disclosed. The following are examples: pledging of assets; other liens; capital stock preferences; interest and amortization provisions pertaining to mortgages, bonds, and other long-term debt; dividend restrictions; obligations to maintain working capital requirements or to reduce debts; and dividend arrearages on preferred stock.

9. *Major commitments.* It is customary to disclose the significant facts regarding major commitments such as the following: pension plans, stock option plans, long-term leases, unutilized letters of credit, abnormally large purchase and sales orders, and commitments for plant acquisition.

10. *Contingencies.* Material contingencies which may result in liabilities or losses should be disclosed. Some examples are: pending or threatened lawsuits, possible additional tax assessments, contested renegotiation claims, guarantees of the debts of others, and notes receivable discounted. Material contingencies which may result in gains or the acquisition of assets should also be disclosed—for example, claims for patent infringement or for reimbursement under price redetermination or condemnation proceedings.

11. *Post-balance sheet events.* Certain events occurring after the balance sheet date must be disclosed if they have a material effect on the company's financial condition and operations. Examples of such events are strikes, major acquisitions or disposals of plant assets, fire losses, and issuance of capital stock.

12. *Unusual and nonrecurring items.* It is customary to disclose and classify separately items which do not relate to the usual or typical operations of the company, such as loans to officers and extra-

ordinary items of profit or loss. Nonrecurring situations and events, by their very nature, are also unusual and likewise call for appropriate disclosure.

13. *Departures from APB Opinions.* Material departures from *Opinions* of the AICPA's Accounting Principles Board are required to be disclosed in statement footnotes or in the auditor's report.

ADEQUACY OF DISCLOSURE—SOME BASIC GUIDES

The phrase *full disclosure* is often loosely used as a synonym for *adequate disclosure*, but it can be mistakenly interpreted to mean that any and all information that anyone could conceivably desire should be disclosed in the financial statements or in the appended notes. Too much disclosure, however, may be just as misleading as too little. The question of excess or insufficiency of disclosure may relate to several features: the type of information furnished, the extent of detail provided for any given item, and the verbiage used. The following discussion presents some of the important guides which may be used by management in the process of selecting appropriate information for disclosure, and by the auditor in carrying out his responsibilities under the third reporting standard.

1. *The statements as overall summarizations.* The financial statements are summarizations of the overall results of the activities of an accounting entity taken as a whole. This basic proposition of accounting immediately establishes certain limits on the types of items to be disclosed. It eliminates the responsibility to report on operations by product, divisions, and other such segments. The emphasis is upon the company *as a whole* and not on its parts.

2. *General-purpose reporting.* Financial reporting, often referred to as general-purpose reporting, is designed to achieve a composite portrayal of the company which can be useful, in a general way, to the several important segments of society who rely upon the financial reports—management, creditors and credit grantors, and stockholders or other investors. Excessively detailed disclosures which one group might welcome may only serve to confuse other groups. Implicit in the concept of general-purpose reporting is the idea that additional supplementary information can be made available by the company itself—in stockholder reports, special reports, conversations with credit grantors, etc.—to meet the special needs of particular groups or specific parties.

3. *Materiality.* The criterion of materiality provides a brake on excessive disclosures and superfluity of detail. The principles of adequate disclosure pertain to matters which are material and significant in the circumstances. Materiality is relative and may depend on the amount of an item or the aggregate of a group of otherwise immaterial items, a relationship to other important accounts or data, current or future significance, normality or abnormality of an occurrence, and expectedness or unexpectedness.

4. *Average prudent investor.* General-purpose reporting is expected to provide impartially for the needs of the several important groups which use financial reports. In recent years, however, accounting literature has placed the greater emphasis on the interests of the investor. The SEC laws and regulations, designed as they are for the protection of investors, were greatly influential in this respect. The SEC, for example, defines *materiality* in Rule 1-02 of Regulation S-X as follows:

> The term "material" when used to qualify a requirement for the furnishing of information as to any subject limits the information required to those matters as to which an average prudent investor ought reasonably to be informed before purchasing the security registered.

In its Supplementary Statement No. 8 (1954) on "Standards of Disclosure for Published Financial Reports," the American Accounting Association, after asserting that the needs of all groups cannot be served equally well by a single set of financial statements, identifies the stockholder group as the primary one. The statement explains that "disclosure is inadequate if interested and informed investors are misled as to any material item." In a later pronouncement ("Accounting and Reporting Standards—1957 Revision"), the AAA states that: "An item should be regarded as material if there is reason to believe that knowledge of it would influence the decisions of an *informed investor*" (italics supplied).

The introduction to Accounting Research Bulletin No. 43 refers in similar vein to a consideration of accounting problems from the standpoint of "the buyer or seller of an interest in an enterprise."

This current emphasis on the investor cannot be fully understood unless an implicit feature is explicitly introduced, namely, that many of the current accounting and reporting problems are particularly important and crucial to large corporations whose stock is publicly held and to their present or future stockholders. It would be a mistake, however, to believe that disclosure standards and requirements ignore the needs of credit grantors, bankers, and other users of financial reports.

5. *Specific circumstances and pressures.* Particularly for small and medium-sized companies, additional information beyond what is normally supplied may be disclosed in the financial statements because of specific circumstances or pressures. A credit grantor, for example, may insist on the inclusion of supplementary schedules including, say, an analysis of the allowance for bad debts or of the collateral supporting the accounts receivable. Long-form reports are often prepared in compliance with such requests. Moreover, specific circumstances surrounding the company—such as a shaky financial condition, the possibility of liquidation, insufficient capital, and similar danger signs—should alert the auditor to the need for fuller disclosures.

6. *General external conditions.* Matters of a widespread nature inherent in the external environment, and which are generally known and affect large segments of society and the economy, need not be disclosed in the financial statements. Such matters or contingencies include business recessions, changes in the tax laws, and the possibility of wars.

7. *Managerial and operational decisions.* It is not customary to disclose decisions dealing with management changes, product changes, unionization, marketing agreements, and other such matters affecting the technical, managerial, and operational conduct of the business. Their financial effect is often doubtful and conjectural. Their disclosure can give rise to misleading inferences and, in revealing confidential information, may be harmful to the company.

8. *Harmful information.* As previously suggested, disclosure of certain kinds of information may be detrimental to the company or its stockholders and, when otherwise unnecessary, should not be revealed. Such caution must be exercised particularly as to research projects and certain details of matters in litigation.

9. *Confidential data.* The auditor often receives confidential information from the client. The disclosure of such information can be harmful to the company but may be of little use to the readers of the report. The auditor must carefully consider whether disclosure of such confidential data is necessary to make the statements not misleading.

10. *Avoidance of verbosity.* Too detailed an explanation or excessive verbiage may be confusing to the reader, who is prevented thereby from identifying and assimilating the essential features of the information presented. Disclosures should be brief and to the point.

11. *Conservatism.* If there is a significant doubt as to whether an item need be disclosed, conservatism will usually influence the auditor to make the disclosure and thus avoid a subsequent claim that the omission resulted in misleading financial statements.

12. *Unusual and nonrecurring items.* As explained in a previous section, such items clearly call for disclosure. They are, by definition, abnormal and as such must be highlighted so that appropriate inferences may be drawn.

13. *Legal requirements.* Some types of disclosures, such as the presentation of the amount of par or stated value capital stock, are made because of legal requirements or legal implications which may be significant to the reader of the report.

14. *Contractual requirements.* Contractual arrangements are often the basis for appropriate disclosures, particularly when they involve the following: long-term commitments such as leases; priorities given to certain parties such as preferred stockholders or creditors who hold prior liens; arrangements which may adversely affect the financial condition of the company; and restrictions on corporate action especially with respect to dividends, acquisition of treasury stock, maintenance of working capital, and the like.

15. *Specific guides in theory and practice.* The foregoing discussions suggest certain general guides and principles on the subject of disclosure. The sources that provide more specific guides are now mentioned.

(a) *AICPA.* The Accounting Research Bulletins, the Statements on Auditing Procedure, the *Opinions* of the Accounting Principles Board, and other literature of the AICPA are replete with examples and illustrations dealing with disclosure requirements, and they should be regarded as authoritative expressions.

(b) *SEC requirements.* Regulation S-X together with the Accounting Series Releases of the SEC state the requirements applicable to the form and content of financial statements which are filed with it. Although some of the disclosure requirements may not correspond to those customarily followed in financial reporting generally, the SEC's rules and regulations can also serve as useful criteria for appraising the adequacy of informative disclosures in financial statements not filed with the Commission.

(c) *New York Stock Exchange.* The *New York Stock Exchange Company Manual* contains, among other matters, the rules and regulations relating to applications for listing on the Exchange. On the matter of statement presentation and disclosures, the manual states that the Exchange does not attempt to prescribe definitely the form or detail of the financial statements included in listing applications, but such statements are expected to be reasonable informative without being overburdened with detail.   In the listing agreement the corporation undertakes, among other things, to submit annual reports to stockholders in which the financial statements are in the same form as the corresponding statements in the listing application and disclose any substantial items of unusual or nonrecurring nature.

(d) *AAA.* The pronouncements of the American Accounting Association have already been referred to, but they must be viewed with caution because many of the points are advanced as ideals for future realization rather than as descriptions of generally accepted practices.

(e) *Robert Morris Associates.* This organization, which is the National Association of Bank Loan Officers and Credit Men, has published a well-known pamphlet entitled *Financial Statements for Bank Credit Purposes.* The pamphlet outlines the financial information the banker would like to see included in accounting reports to assist him in analyzing credit risks. Some of the requested information would more likely be included in a long-form report. But the publication can also be helpful when it is desired to modify the minimum or usual standards of adequate disclosure in order to meet the special requirements of the credit grantor.

(f) *Published reports.* When unusual items arise, or authoritative references are silent or insufficiently informative on a given point, accountants review published annual reports in order to determine the generally accepted practices with respect to the matters in question.

REPORTING ON SUBSEQUENT EVENTS

The subject of reporting on subsequent events is developed in Statement on Auditing Procedures No. 33, Chapter 11. In this section we shall be concerned with classifying such events and with the pertinent disclosure requirements rather than with the auditor's special reporting responsibilities.

Three recognized types of events or transactions occurring subsequent to the balance sheet date are the adjustment accounting group, the future accounting group, and the nonaccounting group. Presented next under each of these types are a description of the group, examples, and disclosure requirements.

1. *Adjustment accounting group.* These are events which directly affect the accounts and financial statements under examination and

call for adjusting journal entries as of the balance sheet date, if not already reflected in the accounts. Some examples are: bankruptcy of a customer where the account was previously considered collectible; settlement of a tax or legal controversy, the outcome and specific amount having been previously indeterminate; and sales of merchandise at depressed prices, thereby affecting inventory valuations at the balance sheet date. These events are disclosed when adjustments are made to reflect them.

2. *Future accounting group.* These are events which are recorded as accounting entries in the *subsequent* period. Some examples are: material gains or losses on sale of such assets as investments and fixed assets; issuance of bonds or capital stock, or contracting for substantial bank loans; major fire losses or other casualties; life insurance proceeds received on death of an officer; and major acquisitions of fixed assets. If material, and particularly if unusual, these events should be disclosed as statement footnotes if disclosure is required to make the statements not misleading.

3. *Nonaccounting group.* These are events which affect the company in a general way and do not lend themselves to specific accounting. Some examples are: loss of a major customer; death of an officer whose unique services had ensured profitable operations; strikes; newly issued government regulations which may seriously affect the industry or company; and major management, product, or operational changes. These events would be disclosed by footnote if material and unusual and if disclosure is required to make the statements not misleading. As a general rule, however, disclosure of nonaccounting events is not required, particularly if: (a) disclosure would not have been made if the events had occurred during the period under examination; (b) the events relate to general business conditions or government regulations which affect the economy or industry as a whole rather than the company alone; and (c) the impact of the events on the particular company is conjectural and indeterminate and, therefore, subject to individual and, perhaps, arbitrary interpretation.

REPORTING RULES FOR PRO FORMA FINANCIAL STATEMENTS

The AICPA's reporting and disclosure rules regarding pro forma financial statements were adopted in 1923. Pro forma financial statements are special-purpose statements which give effect, as of the balance sheet date, to events or transactions which have been consummated or will be in the process of consummation subsequent to that date. The starting point for the preparation of pro forma statements is ordinarily the actual financial statements which are then adjusted to incorporate, hypothetically, the later transactions.

A common type of pro forma statement is a balance sheet which gives effect to a proposed subsequent issue of securities and the application of the proceeds to the acquisition of assets or liquidation of liabilities. Also commonly prepared are pro forma income statements for prior years and a pro forma balance sheet giving effect to combined operations of companies whose merger or other form of business combination is proposed.

The reporting rules, including those pertaining to the auditor's opinion, are as follows:

1. *Definite agreement.* The subsequent transactions must be the subject of a definite agreement, preferably in writing, between the parties. Pro forma statements which give effect simply to contemplated transactions not definitely agreed to, may not be certified.

2. *Capability and responsibility of parties.* The parties must be responsible and also capable of meeting their commitments and obligations. The auditor's opinion must be based on objective, verifiable data. If the transactions have actually been consummated by the date of issuance of the pro forma statements, this requirement is automatically met.

3. *Time factor.* The period of time between the statement date and the expected date of consummation of the future transactions should be reasonably short, say, less than four months. The reasons for this condition relate to concern that: (a) the transactions contemplated may not take place because of intervening events; and (b) other subsequent events may affect the company's operations and financial condition, but since these events are not included in the pro forma statements, misleading inferences may be drawn if only the transactions in question are incorporated.

4. *Due inquiry.* The auditor must make due inquiry and even actual investigation to satisfy himself that in the meantime other transactions or developments have not adversely affected materially the financial position of the company. The usual principles apply for footnote or other disclosures of significant post balance sheet events.

5. *Past tense.* In the description of any financial statements and report thereon, it is desirable to use the past tense so that the reader may know that the report is based on objective data rather than on forecast or conjecture. Obviously, the past tense cannot be used for transactions unconsummated at the report date, but it can be

used to describe the agreements and the steps already taken to carry out the contract.

6. *Disclosure.* Full disclosure, at the heading of the statements and in the report, must be made of the nature of the subsequent transactions, the source of the information used, the major assumptions made, and the purpose for which the statements are issued. The reader must be in a position to understand clearly that the report covers pro forma financial statements and not the usual historical statements.

7. *Opinion.* If the foregoing conditions are met, the auditor can express an opinion on the pro forma statements, but they must be referred to as such. It must be expressly noted also that inasmuch as the pro forma statements are the actual statements adjusted for this purpose, any qualifications which affected an opinion on the actual statements will also apply to an opinion on the pro forma statements.

8. *Forecasts.* Pro forma statements of the type covered by these rules reflect elements of definiteness and objectivity which place them on a plane different from forecasts. The code of professional ethics (Rule No. 2.04) bars the auditor from expressing an opinion on statements containing estimates of future earnings or other forecasts, or creating the belief that he vouches for the accuracy of any forecast. The Committee on Professional Ethics, in Opinion No. 10, indeed, requires the auditor to state that he does not vouch for the accuracy of any forecast. When pro forma statements are certified, the auditor must be certain that they do not contain such forecasts.

9. *SEC rule.* SEC Rule 170 of the General Rules and Regulations under the Securities Act of 1933 prohibits the use of pro forma statements which purport to give effect to the receipt and application of any part of the proceeds from the sale of securities for cash, unless the sale of securities is underwritten and the underwriters are committed either to take and pay for all of the securities or to refund to all subscribers the full amount of subscription payments. The rule also provides that the caption of any pro forma statement must clearly show the assumptions employed. The SEC has a somewhat similar rule under the 1934 Act.

DISCLOSURES IN THE LONG-FORM REPORT

Long-form reports may be submitted to the client by the independent accountant along with the short-form report, or only one report, either short- or long-form, may be submitted. Listed companies receive at least the short-form report which is included in the company's annual report to its stockholders. The information contained in the president's letter and related financial review of the company's annual report to stockholders is similar to that which might be included in a typical long-form report. Long-form reports are submitted primarily for the enlightenment of management which may present them to banks and other credit grantors, at their request, in connection with anticipated borrowings and to facilitate a more precise evaluation of the company's operations and financial condition.

The long-form report contains the same basic financial statements as the short-form report as well as the standard certificate phraseology. It also includes, however, more detailed information by way of textual comments and supplementary schedules and statements. This additional information may relate to the scope of examination or may represent detailed comments on the basic financial statements. In a sense, the long-form report may be viewed as an expansion of the standard certificate and the basic statements. However, the long-form report frequently includes statistical and nonaccounting data which may not necessarily tie in with the basic statements.

Question—November 1951 (6c)

Give four different examples of information which might be contained in an auditor's long-form report but which probably would not appear in the auditor's opinion or in the financial statements or footnotes.

Solution

1. History and organization of the company.

2. Analytical comments and ratios relating to the overall operations and financial condition of the company. Frequently, comparative figures of prior years are presented in this section or in supplementary schedules.

3. Comments and schedules on specific financial statement items. Schedules may provide the details of component items which are reflected in totals on the principal statements, such as sales classified by product, customer, or territory.

4. Statistical data dealing, for example, with inventory quantities or personnel matters (possibly with industry comparisons) which may or may not be related to or tied in with the principal statements.

5. Statements and schedules which tie in with the principal statements, such as those in support of cost of sales, operating expenses, etc.

6. Statement of application of funds, schedule of insurance in force and similar statements and analyses.

INEFFICACY OF DISCLOSURE FOR CURING ACCOUNTING DEFICIENCIES

If the financial statements in a given case are not fair presentations because of deviations from generally accepted accounting principles, mere disclosure of the situation will not cure the deficiencies. If a company, for example, values its inventories at amounts in excess of cost or records fixed assets at arbitrary valuations, it cannot convert unfair statements into fair presentations simply by disclosing the improper practices in notes to financial statements. The purpose of statement notes is to provide additional explanatory information so that the basic fairness of the presentation may be enhanced. The independent accountant must, of course, report in his certificate any accounting deficiencies even if they have already been disclosed by the company in the notes to financial statements. But such disclosures, although helpful, do not really change the financial statements which remain unfair presentations. Consequently, the auditor must appropriately qualify his opinion or submit an adverse opinion unless he can persuade the company to revise the financial statements.

The following is a quotation of some classic expressions on this subject taken from the SEC's Accounting Series Release No. 68 (1949):

> The addition of this footnote did not cure the deficiency . . . . Nor is the mischief cured by an explanatory note revealing that the figure is "purely arbitrary" . . . . Such disclosure, while helpful, is not sufficient . . . . Moreover, even were the footnote to state with complete frankness the true fact that the assets were overvalued, this would not mitigate the effect of the valuation figure itself. A balance-sheet item which is flatly untrue will not be rendered true merely by admission of untruth.

INADEQUATE DISCLOSURE AND THE AUDITOR'S OPINION

A company may sometimes refuse to disclose essential information, the disclosure of which in the financial statement or related notes is necessary for a fair presentation. In such circumstances, according to Statement on Auditing Procedure No. 33, the independent accountant should provide the information in his certificate, usually in a middle paragraph, and then proceed to qualify his opinion.

Statement No. 33 offers the following illustration of the wording of the certificate in instances of inadequate disclosure.

Middle paragraph—material information disclosed

On July 15, 1966, the company issued debentures in the amount of $——— for the purpose of financing plant expansion. The debenture agreement restricts the payment of future cash dividends to earnings after June 30, 1966.

Opinion paragraph—qualified opinion

In our opinion, the accompanying financial statements, except for the omission of the information in the preceding paragraph, present fairly . . . .

Statement No. 33 does not mention the possibility that inadequate disclosure may sometimes necessitate an adverse opinion rather than a qualified opinion. Although disclosure in the certificate does not fully mitigate the effect of lack of disclosure in the financial statements or appended notes, the fact is that disclosure has been made. Consequently, it would appear to be sufficient to qualify the opinion rather than express an adverse opinion. Moreover, the disclosure of an event of the type described in the foregoing illustrative certificate would not in any case involve a modification of the basic form and content of the financial statements. It therefore differs basically from other types of inadequate disclosure which make the statements misleading on their face, such as misclassification of certain noncurrent assets as current, the failure to segregate retained earnings and capital surplus, or the absence of distinction between usual and extraordinary items. Such deficiencies are similar to outright violations of accounting principles in that the accounts themselves—either as to form, classification, or content—are directly involved; hence, material qualifications pertaining to such aspects of inadequate disclosure may lead to an adverse opinion.

A reader of a financial report would certainly have reason to express curiosity at the paradoxical situation which results when, the client having refused to disclose essential information, the auditor proceeds to make such disclosure in so prominent a place as the certificate and, in addition, qualifies his opinion. It would seem that the company has gained nothing in such a situation, and, in fact, is worse off than if it had agreed to appropriate disclosure in the statements or related notes. Admittedly, such situations are rare, but they do occur and they are essentially no different from cases where the company refuses to prepare the statements, in certain material respects, in conformity with general accepted accounting principles.

OFFSET OF ASSETS AND LIABILITIES

In general, the offset of assets and liabilities would represent a violation of accounting principles in that both the asset and liability would be understated. In the event that the offset took the form of a clear disclosure of both the full asset and full liability, the practice would nevertheless constitute a deviation from the standard of adequate disclosure because of the material error in classification.

In ARB No. 43, Chapter 3, it is pointed out that the offset of United States Government securities against the estimated federal tax liability, although a violation of the general rule against offsets, is not so material a matter as to require an exception in the auditor's report. The chief consideration implied here is that the same external party is involved on both the asset and liability side, the securities being regarded as a receivable from the U. S. Government.

When specific assets are pledged to secure certain liabilities, the argument is sometimes advanced that an offset would be proper on the ground that on liquidation the creditor would have a prior right to the pledged asset. In other circumstances, as in the case of the acquisition of real property encumbered by a mortgage, the offset is deemed justified by some as a means of stating the asset at that amount which represents the company's equity in the property. These practices have the effect of understating both the asset and the liability, judged in terms of a going concern, and convey the erroneous impression that it is only the net asset balance which has any significance for the company or outside interests.

STOCKHOLDERS' EQUITY—DISCLOSURE, CLASSIFICATION, AND TERMINOLOGY

As a matter of informative disclosure appropriate captions and terms should be used to describe the *sources* from which the capital of the enterprise was derived.

Question—November 1959 (4)

The total owner's equity (excess of assets over liabilities) is usually shown under a number of subcaptions on the balance sheet of a corporation.

(a) List the major subdivisions of the "stockholders' equity" section of a corporate balance sheet and describe briefly the nature of the amounts that will appear in each section.

(b) Explain fully the reasons for subdividing the amount of stockholders' equity, including legal, accounting, and other considerations.

(c) Describe four different kinds of transactions that will result in paid-in or permanent capital in excess of legal or stated capital.

(d) Various accounting authorities have recommended that the terms "paid-in surplus" and "earned surplus" not be used in published financial statements. Explain briefly the reason for this suggestion, and indicate acceptable substitutes for the terms.

Solution

Major Subdivisions

Accounting Terminology Bulletin No. 1 sets forth the following as major subdivisions of the stockholders' equity section:

1. *Contributed capital:*

(a) *Capital contributed for, or assigned to, shares.* The amounts in this category represent the par or stated value of each class of issued stock.

(b) *Capital surplus.* The more proper term for this category is phraseology similar to the following: *"capital contributed for, or assigned to, shares in excess of par or stated value."* This classification also includes differentials relating to par or stated value in connection with the company's transactions in its own shares.

2. *Retained earnings.* Retained earnings represents accumulated profits retained in the business. Appropriations of retained earnings may be separately stated as surplus reserves or disclosed in statement footnotes.

3. *Appraisal surplus.* Asset appreciation based on appraisal values are credited to this account, but the practice of recording asset appreciation, it should be noted, is generally a violation of accepted accounting principles.

4. *Treasury stock.* This category includes the cost of the company's stock held in the treasury and not cancelled or reissued.

Reasons for Equity Classifications

Stockholders' equity is so subdivided for the following reasons:

1. *Source.* Distinction between contributed capital and retained earnings is maintained to show the extent to which growth was financed by contributed capital, appraisal increase, earnings, etc.

2. *Interests.* The relative equity interests of the different classes of owners are more clearly revealed by disclosures of classes of stock and dividend and other preferences.

3. *Restrictions.* Classifications are also designed to highlight restrictions. The laws of many states, for example, consider the capital contributed for the par or stated value of issued shares to be "legal capital" in the nature of a trust fund for the benefit of creditors, not to be impaired by dividend payments or acquisition of treasury stock Such impairment would arise if these transactions would result in a diminution of legal capital.

4. *Return of capital.* The separate classification of contributed capital and earned capital (retained earnings) serves to distinguish dividends out of earnings from distributions which are a return of capital. The distinction between retained earnings and contributed capital, moreover, provides a guide for determining the amount of dividends that may be distributed to stockholders. State corporation laws vary in this connection, a divided distribution out of capital surplus being permitted in some states.

Sources of Capital Surplus

Contributed capital in excess of par or stated value may originate as follows.

1. *Price.* The issuance of shares at a price which exceeds the par or stated value of the shares.

2. *Stock dividend.* The capitalized difference between the par value and fair value of shares issued as a stock dividend.

3. *Treasury stock transactions.* The excess of proceeds from sale of treasury stock over cost thereof or the excess of par or stated value over the cost of treasury shares retired.

4. *Donated assets.* Contributions of assets to a corporation.

5. *Forfeited subscriptions.* Amounts received on forfeited stock subscriptions which are not refunded to the subscriber.

6. *Reorganizations.* Reorganizations, quasi-reorganizations, recapitalizations, conversion of bonded indebtedness, mergers, etc.

Use of the Term Surplus

1. *The idea of excess.* Whether used in the account "Capital (or Paid-In Surplus) Surplus" or the account "Earned Surplus," the term surplus connotes to the layman something that is in excess and, therefore, is not needed. This is an erroneous conception and a change in terminology is needed to avoid this misinterpretation.

2. *Dividends.* The term *surplus* may also suggest, particularly for retained earnings, that the entire amount of the account which bears the term is available for the payment of dividends or for other stockholder distribution.

3. *Multiple use.* Another added source of confusion has been the use of the term for a variety of accounts such as "earned surplus," "capital surplus," and "appraisal surplus."

4. *Established meanings.* The terms *surplus* and *capital surplus* have meanings in other fields such as economics and law which differ from those intended to be expressed in accounting. The substitution of more appropriate terms would help to eliminate this misunderstanding.

5. *Recommended terminology.* The AICPA in Accounting Terminology Bulletin No. 1 recommends that the use of the term surplus be discontinued and that substitute terminology similar to the following be employed: in place of earned surplus—retained income, retained earnings, or earnings retained for use in the business; in place of capital surplus—capital contributed in excess of par or stated value; in place of donated surplus—capital received other than for shares; in place of appraisal surplus—excess of appraised value of fixed assets over cost.

TYPES OF RESERVES

The term *reserve* has been customarily used in accounting in a variety of senses which are necessarily conflicting, and this has given rise to misunderstanding in the interpretation of financial statements.

QUESTION—November 1946 (9)

Probably no other term used by accountants is required to do duty in so many capacities as the word "reserve." Describe briefly four distinct accounting meanings or uses of this term.

Solution

1. *Valuation reserve.* This type of reserve takes the form of a deduction from an asset in order to state the asset at its realizable amount or on an amortized basis, as in the case of the allowance for bad debts or allowance for depreciation.

2. *Estimated liability.* An estimated liability, as in the case of an estimated accrual for warranty costs or the estimated liability for Federal income taxes, is often referred to as a reserve.

3. *Surplus reserve.* An appropriation of retained earnings, such as a reserve for possible future losses or for plant expansion, is similarly referred to as a reserve.

4. *Income charges.* Less frequently referred to as reserves are the charges to income for such items as bad debts or depreciation. These correspond to the offsetting credits to valuation accounts which, as noted, are similarly sometimes viewed as reserves.

5. *Appraisal surplus.* Credits for unrealized appraisal increases in the amounts at which assets are stated are sometimes given a title such as "reserve for unrealized appraisal increments."

6. *Unrealized income.* Deferred gross profit and similar unrealized income accounts are sometimes designated as reserve accounts.

7. *Secret reserves.* A "secret reserve" arises when there is a deliberate attempt to understate the net assets and income of a company through undervaluation of inventories, excessive depreciation rates, and similar methods.

USE OF THE TERM RESERVE

The AICPA, in Accounting Terminology Bulletin No. 1, recommends that the term *reserve* be used only when referring to surplus reserves. Hence, terms such as "reserve for depreciation," "reserve for bad debts," and "reserve for Federal income taxes" would be replaced by appropriate account titles such as "allowance for bad debts," "estimated liability for Federal income taxes," and the like. Others have advocated that the term *reserve* be eliminated entirely and not used even to describe an appropriation of retained earnings. The following are some points advanced by those who advocate that the term *reserve* be entirely eliminated.

1. *Fund.* The term reserve, in whatever sense used, implies that a fund has been set aside for some purpose. In supporting the retention of the term for surplus reserves, the AICPA suggested that this was justified because a portion of net assets, although unidentified

and undivided, was being retained for a special purpose as in the case of a reserve for plant expansion. But even here no actual fund has been created.

2. *Dividend restrictions.* Surplus reserves are often used as a means of alleviating stockholder pressure for dividends or as a means of achieving self-restraint with respect to dividend or other distributions. The erroneous impression can be created, however, that the unappropriated balance of retained earnings is currently available in full for the payment of dividends.

3. *Disclosure.* Surplus reserves are often used as a means of disclosing a contingency or management policy, but such information can just as well be provided in footnotes to financial statements.

4. *Contingencies.* The use of surplus reserves can sometimes be used to justify the failure to decide whether a contingency is such that a liability should in fact be recorded. The disclosure of the situation as a surplus reserve would not be a proper substitute in such circumstances.

5. *Legal requirements.* In the event that an appropriation of retained earnings is required by state law or contract, a surplus reserve must, of course, be recorded. But even in this circumstance the account need not carry the term *reserve* in the title.

6. *Segment of retained earnings.* A surplus reserve is simply a portion of retained earnings. Its nature in this respect can be clearly indicated by placing it with unappropriated retained earnings and then providing a caption for total retained earnings.

RESERVES, CONTINGENCIES, AND THE "TWILIGHT ZONE"

It is frequently difficult to decide whether a particular contingency warrants recording as a liability or simply disclosure by way of a footnote or the establishment of a surplus reserve. Some companies resolve this problem by showing reserves in what has been referred to as the "twilight zone," the section of the balance sheet between liabilities and capital.

Question—November 1951 (3)

It has been proposed that the "reserves" section on the liability side of the balance sheet be eliminated and that all such reserves be classified either as liabilities or as part of the stockholders' equity. Give the arguments for and against this proposal.

Solution

1. *Different types.* The reserve section on the liability side of the balance sheet may be improperly used as a catch-all for different types of reserves—liability, surplus, and even, most improperly, valuation reserves. It is therefore desirable that this section be eliminated and the accounts be shown where they properly belong.

2. *Origin of credits.* The credits to the various reserve accounts may have originated in different ways. Thus a liability reserve would have been recorded by an offsetting charge to income; a surplus reserve by a charge to retained earnings. This distinction is decisive in categorizing the reserve either as an estimated liability or as an appropriation of retained earnings. The reader of the statements should be left in no doubt as to the nature or origin of the reserve account, and this enlightenment can only be achieved when the reserve section has been eliminated.

3. *Uncertainties.* The factor of uncertainty may extend to such matters as lawsuits, uncompleted transactions, renegotiation matters, and warranties. Management may look upon the reserve section as a practical solution when it is difficult for it to decide whether or not the uncertainties surrounding a contingency would permit reasonable estimates to be made regarding the occurrence of a liability and the amounts to be recorded.

4. *Accounting judgment.* If a reserve is set up by a charge to income, this would automatically mean that a liability reserve was intended, thus warranting its inclusion in the liability section. If retained earnings were charged, this would signify that a surplus reserve was being created, and that account would then have to be shown in the capital section. Hence, the anomalous reserve section does not provide a fair presentation of the reserve accounts unless it is used as a means of suggesting to the reader (when, for example, a liability reserve has been created) that a liability either may not actually materialize or the ultimate amount may be lower than the recorded figure. The reader, however, could find this confusing and, in any event, should not have to bear the burden of making an accounting judgment of this nature.

CONTINGENT LIABILITY

Contingent liabilities is the term which is offered most popularly as an illustration of contingencies, but more properly it is to be regarded as a subclassification of the latter. A definition of contingent liabilities and the methods of disclosure are presented in the following discussion.

1. *Existing conditions.* A contingent liability relates to factors or conditions existing at the balance sheet date which may later develop into an actual liability and corresponding loss (for example, pending lawsuit). A contingent liability should be distinguished from a *contingent loss* which is the term used to refer to the possibility of a loss (from fire or other catastrophies, for example) resulting from an event unrelated to factors or conditions existing at the balance sheet date.

2. *Questionable assets.* The conditions may develop into an actual liability with corresponding acquisition of an asset of questionable value (for example, notes discounted, if dishonored, will give rise to claim against, and receivable from, the maker whose credit standing would be questionable).

3. *Commitments.* There may be continuing commitments involving irreducible overhead costs (for example, long-term lease commitments which must be met despite decline in prevailing rentals and inability of company to bear the burdensome rentals).

4. *Losses.* The conditions may result in actual loss or in reduction in expected profits (for example, inventories in excess of reasonable requirements, the profitability of which on ultimate disposal is not reasonably determinable because realization will take place considerably in the future).

5. *Amounts.* The amount of possible future loss or liability may or may not be determinable, although sometimes, as in lawsuits, the maximum possible loss may be known.

6. *Uncertainty.* The uncertainty as to whether an actual liability or loss will take place is an essential feature of most types of contingent liabilities.

7. *Estimates.* Generally accepted accounting principles require that an estimated liability be recorded at the statement date if there is a reasonable probability that the company will later incur costs, expenses, or losses, which, as in the case of product warranties, are clearly identifiable with the current period. The estimated liability so recorded is a known liability despite the element of estimate regarding the amount to be recorded. Situations of this type should be distinguished from a contingent liability which may be said to exist because of the possibility that the actual future costs or losses may be considerably in excess of the estimated amounts recorded as of the statement date.

8. *Statement presentation.* Contingent liabilities may be disclosed in the financial statements as follows:

(a) By notation under a caption entitled "contingent liabilities" in the space between the liability and capital sections of the balance sheet.

(b) By inclusion in notes to financial statements either at the bottom of the balance sheet or in appended notes.

(c) By informative description of a surplus reserve established because of the contingent liability.

(d) By informative description of an offset against the related asset, for example, notes receivable discounted deducted from notes receivable.

ACCOUNTING FOR CONTINGENCIES

The subject of contingencies and contingency reserves is considered by the AICPA in ARB No. 43, Chapter 6, entitled "Contingency Reserves," and in ARB No. 50, entitled "Contingencies." The accounting and reporting principles set forth in these bulletins are summarized below.

1. *Definition of contingency.* A contingency is a condition or circumstance existing at the balance sheet date which may result in the future in the acquisition or loss of an asset, a liability, or avoidance of a liability, and ususlly with a gain or loss resulting. The occurrence of the future event which would result in these effects is fraught with considerable uncertainty.

2. *Recording.* Because the outcome of contingencies cannot be reasonably predicted, no account entries are made; but if the circumstances can materially affect the company's position, appropriate disclosure should be made.

3. *Adverse contingencies.* The following are examples of adverse contingencies which can result in future charges to income: pending lawsuits, possible assessments of additional taxes, and guarantees.

4. *Contingent gains.* Some examples of contingencies which can result in gains are lawsuits against others and renegotiations. Material contingencies of this type should also be disclosed.

5. *Actual liability.* If the outcome of a contingency relating to conditions existing at the balance sheet date is reasonably foreseeable, and will result in a loss, both the loss and liability should be recorded. However, if gains are involved in such circumstances, no entry would

be made on the ground that no income is to be recorded prior to realization.

6. *Method of disclosure.* Contingencies should be disclosed in notes to financial statements which should indicate the nature of the contingency and the outlook and provide, if feasible, an estimate of the amounts involved or explain why an estimate cannot be determined.

7. *Commitments and other situations.* Certain commitments and other situations for which disclosure is frequently made have sometimes improperly been described as contingencies. Some examples are: unutilized letters of credit, dividends in arrears, long-term leases, and bond indenture or other contractual restrictions regarding maintenance of working capital and acquisition of capital stock.

8. *Contingency reserve.* A contingency reserve is a surplus reserve created out of retained earnings in anticipation of losses or other unfavorable contingencies which might arise in the future.

9. *Manipulation of income.* Contingency reserves must be restored to retained earnings when no longer considered necessary by the company. Neither their creation nor their restoration to retained earnings has any effect on income. It would be improper to use these reserves in order to manipulate income or to shift income between accounting periods. An example of an improper practice is to charge an income or an expense account in setting up the reserve. Another misrepresentation would be the charge of an actual loss to the reserve account in a future period. This would have the effect of relieving the income account of subsequent periods.

EFFECT OF CONTINGENCIES AND UNUSUAL UNCERTAINTIES ON THE AUDITOR'S OPINION

If there are unusual uncertainties as to the effect of future developments on certain items affecting the financial position and results of operations of a company, the auditor may find it necessary to qualify his opinion or, if the exceptions are sufficiently material, to submit a disclaimer of opinion. The following is a summary of the reporting principles pertinent to this subject, based in part on the discussion in Statement on Auditing Procedure No. 33.

1. *Reason for qualification or disclaimer.* Because the probable effects of the matter in question are not determinable at the time the report is submitted, the auditor is unable to express an unqualified

opinion on the fairness of the financial statements. There is some element of similarity here to those cases in which a limited scope of examination precludes the auditor from acquiring sufficient information to enable him to express an unqualified opinion. The significant difference is, of course, that the unusual uncertainties, and the lack of sufficient knowledge as to the outcome, are inherent in the particular circumstances. And, although the effect seems to be the same, a report containing a qualified opinion or a disclaimer resulting from such uncertainties is certainly more useful to the reader than one in which the opinion is affected by a limited examination.

2. *Examples of unusual uncertainties.* Some situations of unusual uncertainty are dependent for their final outcome upon the decisions of persons other than management. Certain lawsuits, tax matters, and other contingencies are some examples. In other cases, the uncertainties may involve the judgment or decision of management, for example, questions of valuation or realizability of assets.

3. *Characteristics.* The element of uncertainty permeates many of the transactions and events which accounting seeks to portray, but this factor does not usually prevent a company from exercising its best judgment in arriving at reasonable estimates and conclusions in conformity with acceptable accounting principles and methods. The computation of depreciation allowances, estimated bad debts, or liability reserves entails an awareness of uncertainties, but these are not the type of circumstances to which this discussion is directed. The uncertainties under present discussion have the following characteristics:

(a) The circumstances and the attendant uncertainties must be unusual.

(b) The uncertainties must arise from the character of the circumstances rather than from any hesitation or lack of confidence in assuming the responsibility to exercise proper accounting judgment.

(c) The generally accepted accounting concepts, principles, methods and rules—particularly insofar as they are designed to deal with uncertainties—cannot provide the necessary guidance to deal with the problem because of the nature of the circumstances.

(d) Reasonable judgments cannot be made.

(e) The probable effects are material.

The following illustrations of the effect on the wording of the opinion paragraph are drawn from Statement No. 33. The first example is a qualified opinion based on inability to determine the extent of the company's tax liability.

Illustration No. 1—qualified opinion

In our opinion, subject to any adjustments to the balance sheet and statement of retained earnings which may result from the final determination of the company's income tax liability for prior years as indicated in Note A to the financial statements, the accompanying financial statements present fairly . . . .

A qualified opinion should normally contain a phrase like "except" or "exception" but the phrase, "subject to," as used in the first and second illustrations, is appropriate when the qualification is based on unusual uncertainties.

Illustration No. 2—qualified opinion

In our opinion, subject to the successful conclusion of B project and the ultimate recovery thereby of the related deferred research and development costs in the amount of $——— described in Note C to the financial statements, the accompanying financial statements present fairly . . . .

The final illustration is one in which a disclaimer of opinion is expressed because of the extreme materiality of the amounts in question. The opinion paragraph makes reference to the middle paragraph of the certificate in which the facts are described, but the data could equally as well have been provided in a note to the financial statements to which similar reference could have been made in the disclaimer.

Illustration No. 3—disclaimer of opinion

Because of the possible material effect on the financial statements of the above-mentioned lawsuit, the outcome of which is uncertain, we do not express any opinion on the company's financial statements taken as a whole.

CONSISTENCY STANDARD

The meaning of consistency and its importance as a major accounting concept were elaborated upon in Chapter 1. In this chapter our emphasis will be upon its reporting implications and on the associated concept of comparability.

The second reporting standard of the generally accepted auditing standards requires that the auditor state in his report whether the principles of accounting have been consistently observed in the current period in relation to the preceding accounting period. The following is a discussion of the objective of the consistency standard.

1. *Comparability.* The consistency standard provides assurance that, unless otherwise disclosed, the comparability of the financial statements as between periods has not been affected by changes in accounting principles or methods.

2. *Disclosure.* If a change in accounting methods has materially affected the comparability of financial statements, the company must disclose the facts of the change and its effect on the statements. The consistency standard requires that the auditor review the adequacy and informativeness of these disclosures. If the company has not reported the inconsistency and its effects in a note to its financial statements, such disclosure must be made by the auditor in a middle paragraph of the certificate. In any case, the opinion paragraph is appropriately modified.

3. *Alternative methods.* Alternative accounting methods may be equally acceptable. Were it not for the consistency standard, the auditor's report would take no cognizance of the effect of a change in method as long as the method selected was in conformity with generally accepted accounting principles.

4. *Shifting of income.* The standard acts as a deterrent to arbitrary or continuous changes in accounting methods in order to shift income from one period to another at the whim of management.

5. *Improper and misleading conclusions.* In general, the concept of consistency and the applicable reporting rules ensure that the reader of the accountant's report will not draw improper and misleading conclusions because of an inconsistency in the application of accounting principles.

REPORTING ON INCONSISTENCY

The following rules for reporting on inconsistency involve the responsibilities of both management and the independent accountant.

1. *Change in accounting principles.* An inconsistency arises if there has been a change in accounting principles and practices or in the methods of applying them.

2. *Choice of principles.* This type of change involves a choice by management of a principle or method from among alternatively acceptable principles or methods.

3. *Examples.* A change from Lifo to Fifo or from straight-line to declining-balance depreciation constitutes an inconsistency.

4. *Materiality.* The opinion paragraph is affected if the change has a material effect on the earnings or financial position.

5. *Current immateriality but material future effect.* If an inconsistency has an immaterial effect in the current year, but is expected to have a material effect in later years, the change should be described in a note to the financial statements (or, in the absence of such note, in a comment paragraph of the certificate) but no reference to it is required, or should be made, in the opinion paragraph.

6. *Disclosure.* The change and its effect should be adequately described either in a note to financial statements (preferably, because the financial statements are the representations of management which has the basic and primary responsibility for their accuracy and for the selection of appropriate accounting principles) or (alternatively acceptable) in a comment paragraph of the certificate. The following matters must be disclosed:

(a) Description of the change.

(b) The effect on the balance sheet.

(c) The effect on the income statement, including the amount by which net income is affected after consideration of related income taxes.

7. *Effect on opinion.* The opinion paragraph must refer to the note to financial statements (or to the comment paragraph) which describes the change and its effects. But see item (10) below.

8. *Example of wording.* The affected part of the opinion paragraph would read somewhat as follows:

> . . . in conformity with generally accepted accounting principles which, except for the change, which we approve, in pricing of inventories as described in Note 4 to the financial statements [or, as described in the preceding paragraph,] have been applied on a basis consistent with that of the preceding year.

9. *Indication of approval.* If the change has been made from an acceptable method to another acceptable method, the auditor need not indicate that he approves of the change. Such approval is implied in view of the absence of a qualification as to the fairness of presentation. Nevertheless, the auditor may indicate his approval if he so desires. If the change has been from an unacceptable to an acceptable principle, he will ordinarily wish to express his approval of the change. In filings with the SEC, however, the auditor's opinion of

the change must be given in accordance with the requirement of Rule 2-02 of Regulation S-X.

10. *Qualification as to consistency.* The reference in the opinion paragraph to an inconsistency is often referred to as a *qualification as to consistency.* The phraseology is unfortunate because it can be misinterpreted as signifying a qualified opinion. A qualification as to consistency is actually an *explanation* as to consistency in the opinion paragraph and is not a qualified opinion. The opinion paragraph may be thus modified for reporting on an inconsistency and yet the overall opinion itself is unqualified.

11. *Qualified or adverse opinion.* If there has been a change to an unacceptable accounting principle or the change has been made in order to shift income arbitrarily between periods or, in general, if violations of accounting principles or reporting standards are involved, the change will evoke the larger issues of fairness of presentation and not simply consistency. In such circumstances, the auditor would be required to express either a qualified opinion or, if sufficiently material, an adverse opinion on the financial statements as a whole.

THE MEANING OF COMPARABILITY—REPORTING RULES

Lack of consistency affects comparability, but a lack of comparability may be caused by factors other than inconsistency. The concept of comparability is of fundamental importance in accounting and auditing. Business decisions and the effective use of financial statements necessarily involve comparisons of the financial condition and earnings of a single company from period to period, and of one company with others in the same or different industries.

The comparability of financial statements may be affected either by underlying conditions or by accounting practices. The following is an exposition of the factors which may enhance or detract from the comparability of intercompany or interperiod financial statements.

Intercompany Comparability

1. *Uniformity in accounting.* Adherence to generally accepted accounting principles ensures the comparability of financial statements among companies. But uniformity in accounting does not mean that the accounting methods used in applying these broad principles must be uniform or that uniformity should be used to disguise essential differences.

2. *Accounting methods.* If comparability is to be achieved, the

accounting methods must also be generally accepted. But the availability of equally acceptable alternative methods makes it possible to apply broad accounting principles to the individual circumstances of a particular company. The existence of such choice is particularly important for the exercise of sound judgment on matters which entail elements of uncertainty, indefiniteness, estimate, interpretation, and conservatism. One enterprise may adopt the declining-balance method of depreciation, and another the straight-line method, but both will be applying the broad principle of writing off the depreciable assets over their useful lives. Some accountants believe that comparability is affected unless all companies adopt not only uniform broad principles but also uniform accounting methods. Although it is true that in many areas of accounting, alternative methods can be freely chosen regardless of individual circumstances (for example, Lifo and Fifo, declining-balance and straight-line depreciation methods, etc.), the adopted method does reflect an accounting judgment as to an appropriate application of a broad principle.

3. *Price-level changes.* Some accountants believe that price-level accounting will provide greater intercompany and interperiod comparability than the generally accepted historical-cost basis of accounting. The AICPA has taken the position (in Chapter 9, Accounting Research Bulletin No. 43) that any such change in the basic structure of accounting would be inadvisable at this time, but it gives its support to the use of supplementary financial schedules for the disclosure of the effects of price-level changes on the financial statements.

4. *Form versus substance.* Intercompany comparability may be affected if transactions or events similar in economic substance are accounted for differently simply because they are different in form. A classic example of this is the current controversial problem of accounting for leases, particularly long-term leases. The AICPA (in APB Opinion No. 5) requires disclosure of rental obligations and other important data with respect to long-term leases, and even recommends the recording of the asset and corresponding liabilities if the transaction is in substance a purchase. Some accountants would go much further and, contrary to the AICPA position, propose that all long-term leases (whether or not they are purchases in substance) be capitalized at the present value of the total rentals, along with the corresponding liabilities. In general, the question of what is form and what is substance frequently arises in accounting and is a reflection of the complexity of the economic environment with which accounting deals.

5. *Clear-cut criteria.* In a number of accounting areas, intercom-

pany (and even interperiod) comparability may be affected depending on the definiteness of the established criteria for making consistent accounting judgments. Often cited as illustrations of the adverse effect of a lack of clear-cut criteria and the consequent diversity in accounting and reporting practices are the problems of the inclusion or exclusion from income of material extraordinary items of profit and loss (considered in Accounting Research Bulletin No. 43, Chapter 8) and of the treatment of a business combination as a purchase or a pooling (discussed in Accounting Research Bulletin No. 48).

6. *Interperiod changes.* The factors to be discussed, such as changes in accounting methods or changed conditions, that affect the interperiod comparability of financial statements for an individual company, similarly affect the comparability of that company with other enterprises.

Interperiod Comparability

Statement on Auditing Procedure No. 33, in clarifying the relationship between consistency and comparability, focuses its attention on interperiod comparability. It describes four classes of factors which may produce a lack of comparability.

1. *Inconsistency—changes in accounting principles.* This is the only one of the four classes affecting interperiod comparability which involves the consistency standard and therefore requires recognition in the auditor's opinion as to consistency.

2. *Changed conditions—changes in accounting but not in accounting principles.* The characteristics of this class and the reporting rules may be summarized as follows:

(a) *Altered conditions.* An accounting change, but not a change in accounting principles or methods, is required by altered conditions.

(b) *Accounting change versus change in accounting method.* The term *accounting change* means a change in the factors which enter into an accounting computation, but the same accounting method continues to be used.

(c) *Examples.* A change in the estimated remaining useful life of fixed assets because of obsolescence or other circumstances (for example, altered conditions) will necessitate a change in depreciation rate (that is, an accounting change), but the same accounting method, say the straight-line basis, will continue to be used. Another example is a change in the percentage applied to accounts receivable to arrive at the estimated allowance for bad debts. Altered circumstances pertaining to the collectibility of the accounts and reevaluation of bad debts experience formed the basis for the accounting change, but the basic accounting principle or method was unchanged. Of similar nature is a change in the periodic accrual of costs of a pension plan resulting from revisions in actuarial assumptions.

(d) *Absence of choice.* Unlike an inconsistency, no change in accounting principles is involved and, hence, management has made no choice in this respect. The company must, of course, exercise sound judgment relative to the factors involved in the accounting computation.

(e) *Disclosure.* If this type of change has a material effect on the financial statements, it will affect comparability. The company is therefore obligated to disclose the circumstances and effect of the change in a note to the financial statements.

(f) *No effect on opinion.* The change is not an inconsistency. It therefore does not affect the auditor's opinion as to consistency, and no mention of the change should be made in the opinion paragraph. The auditor will ordinarily not refer to it in a comment paragraph of the certificate, but may sometimes wish to do so as a matter of informative disclosure.

(g) *SEC rule.* The SEC requires (in Rule 2-02, Regulation S-X) that the independent accountant disclose in his report and express his opinion of any material changes in accounting principles or practices or methods of applying them which affect comparability, or any material retroactive adjustments of the accounts. If an actual inconsistency is involved (as in class 1), this requirement may be met by appropriate wording in the opinion paragraph. But for an accounting change which is technically not an inconsistency (as in class 2), a description of the change and the auditor's opinion thereon expressed in a middle comment paragraph (not the opinion paragraph) should fulfill the SEC requirements for reports filed with it.

3. *Changed conditions—new happenings resulting in accounting effects but no change in accounting principles.* The following are the characteristics and reporting rules of this class:

(a) *Specific happening.* Changes of this type take the form of a specific happening or transaction.

(b) *New situation.* The event constitutes an essentially new situation.

(c) *Accounting effect versus change in accounting method.* The happening has an accounting effect but, because of the newness of the happening, entails the selection of an accounting method or practice for the first time, rather than a change in method.

(d) *Examples.* The acquisition or disposal of a subsidiary or plant and the initial adoption of a pension plan are examples of this class of change which does affect the comparability of financial statements. An additional example might be a new type of fixed asset acquired that has a useful life of, say, five years, whereas formerly owned fixed assets may have been depreciated over ten years. In previous years, sales were made on a regular accrual basis. In the current year, an installment sales department was established with sales for that department to be reported on an installment basis. In none of these examples has there been any inconsistency, that is, any *change* in accounting principles.

(e) *Disclosure.* A material "change" of this type affects comparability and may require disclosure in notes to financial statements. Certain important events of this kind are, in any event, traditionally disclosed in statement footnotes. Some new situations, like the example dealing with installment sales, may not require footnote disclosure since they are automatically disclosed directly in the financial statements, as in the presentation of installment sales and deferred gross profit accounts.

(f) *No effect on opinion.* The change is not an inconsistency. It therefore does not affect the auditor's opinion as to consistency, and no mention of the change should be made in the opinion paragraph. If the auditor were to comment upon the event in a comment paragraph of the certificate, he would do so only as a matter of informative disclosure, but, for this type of change, such reference in the report would be made only in unusual circumstances.

4. *Reclassifications.* Reclassifications of items in the financial statements will obviously affect comparability. The following considerations apply to this type of change:

(a) *Significance of change.* Reclassifications are usually not important because ordinarily they do not affect net income. But in certain circumstances the change may be material.

(b) *Examples.* Freight out, formerly deducted from sales revenue, may be reclassified as an operating expense. Unamortized bond discount, previously presented as an asset, may be reclassified as a deduction from bonds payable. United States government securities may be applied, for the first time, against the federal income tax liability.

(c) *Disclosure.* Statement on Auditing Procedure No. 33 states that reclassifications are not usually important enough to be disclosed. Material changes in classification, however, should be explained in the financial statements or notes but need not ordinarily be referred to in the certificate.

(d) *No effect on opinion.* The implication seems to be that a reclassification is not really a change in accounting principles. It is not an inconsistency and therefore requires no reference in the opinion paragraph. It would seem, however, that a combination of factors—including the effect on net income, materiality, pervasiveness of the reclassification, and the possibility of misleading inferences— may, in the particular circumstances and in the judgment of the auditor, warrant that he view the reclassification as an inconsistency to be commented upon in the opinion paragraph.

COMPARATIVE STATEMENTS

In ARB No. 43, Chapter 2, the Committee on Accounting Procedure expresses a preference for the issuance by corporations of comparative statements (current year and one or more preceding years) rather than statements of a single year. It is a common practice for corporations to include as part of their annual report a summary of earnings for the last ten years. Registration statements filed with the Securities and Exchange Commission call for financial data for a five-year period.

Question—May 1964 (2)

Financial statement analysis and interpretation is an integral part of the accounting function. Comparative financial position and operating statements are commonly used tools of analysis and interpretation.

(a) Discuss the inherent limitations of single-year statements for purposes of analysis and interpretation. Include in your discussion the extent to which these limitations are overcome by the use of comparative statements.

(b) Comparative balance sheets and comparative income statements that show a firm's financial history for each of the last ten years may be misleading. Discuss the factors or conditions that might contribute to misinterpretations. Include a discussion of the additional information and supplementary data that might be included in or provided with the statements to prevent misinterpretations.

Solution

Usefulness of Comparative Statements

1. *Limitations.* Single-year statements cover a very short period in the life of a business and are therefore, in a sense, "interim state-

ments." Comparative reports showing two or more periods provide a more informative basis for evaluating the results of operations and also convey the message that performance measures covering a number of years are more significant than the operating results of a single year.

2. *Trends.* Comparative statements provide a basis for viewing trends in performance as well as changes in the financial position of a firm over a period of time.

3. *Funds.* Comparative balance sheets are necessary for the determination of sources and applications of funds.

4. *Allocations.* Financial statements are based on allocations of revenues and expenses as between accounting periods. Allocation errors involving deferrals or accruals of income and expense are more likely to distort the operations of a single year than of a series of years.

5. *Abnormality.* The financial statements of a single year are affected by many economic influences, and as a result may not be representative of the normal operations of the company.

6. *Management.* Comparative statements serve to focus management's attention on variations from year to year, thereby facilitating evaluation and control.

Additional Information

1. *Consistency and comparability.* Any change in method or other cause of lack of comparability should be disclosed.

2. *Prior notes.* Any footnotes or explanations which were appended to prior years' statements should be repeated in the comparative statements to the extent that they are still significant.

3. *Reclassification.* Reclassifications may affect comparability and similarly should be disclosed.

4. *Price level.* Supplementary data may be necessary in the event that price-level changes affect the comparability of financial statements. The statements based on historical cost can be adjusted in the supplementary statements to show the impact of price-level changes.

5. *Nonrecurring events.* Such events can distort the comparability of comparative statements unless they are properly noted.

6. *Enterprise changes.* Modifications of corporate structure and of business practices, including changes in products, subsidiary affiliations and the like, can greatly affect the reader's capacity to compare the operating results over a span of years.

CONSISTENCY AND COMPARATIVE STATEMENTS

In reporting on inconsistency when comparative statements for two or more years are included in the report, the rules which apply, as stated in Statement on Auditing Procedure No. 33, vary somewhat depending on whether the comparative statements of prior years have been restated after retroactive adjustment. These rules may be said to govern management's reporting responsibilities where they refer to disclosures in the financial statements and accompanying notes, and the auditor's reporting responsibilities where reference is made to the opinion.

Prior Years Not Restated

1. *Basic principle.* The basic principle underlying the consistency standard is its concern with the comparability of the financial statements of the current and preceding year (even if the preceding year's statements are not included in the report), and of all years presented in the report in comparative form.

2. *Change in current year.* If the change occurs in the current year, it should be appropriately disclosed in a note to financial statements and, in addition, should be referred to in the opinion paragraph in accordance with the usual rules for reporting on inconsistency. This rule applies to a report on the current year alone or on financial statements presented in comparative form.

3. *Change in prior year.* If the change occurred in a year prior to the current year, and the year of change is included in the comparative statements, the following reporting requirements apply:

(a) *Opinion only on current year.* If the opinion is only on the current year, no reference need be made in the opinion paragraph, but suitable disclosure should be made in a note appended to the financial statements of the year of change.

(b) *Opinion on all included years.* If the auditor is reporting on all the years, he should refer in the opinion paragraph to a note to the financial statements which describes the change and its effect.

Prior Years Restated

4. *Effect of restatement.* If a company has changed an accounting method in the current year but regards the change as one which retroactively applies to prior years, management would normally find it

desirable to provide restated comparative statements for a reasonable number of past periods affected. A restatement of the financial information for such prior years places all periods, including the current year, on a comparable basis.

5. *Change in current year.* If the change took place in the current year, the following reporting requirements apply:

(a) *Opinion only on current year.* If the auditor is reporting only on the current year, he must refer to the change in the opinion paragraph in accordance with the usual rules on reporting an inconsistency. The description and effect of the change and the facts regarding the retroactive adjustment should be disclosed in notes to the financial statements.

(b) *Opinion on all included years.* If the auditor is reporting on all the restated years (including, of course, the current year), appropriate disclosure should be made in notes to the financial statements. In addition, and even though all years included in the report are on a consistent basis in view of the retroactive restatement, the opinion paragraph should refer to the restatement.

6. *Change in prior year.* If the change occurred in a year prior to the current year, there is no need to make any reference to this in the certificate. But if any of the comparative financial statements included in the report have been restated, disclosure of the change should be made in the notes to financial statements relating to such restated years.

Pooling of Interests

7. *Nature of pooling.* The AICPA's position on the accounting for business combinations is set forth in Accounting Research Bulletin No. 48. A pooling of interests (as contrasted with a purchase) is a business combination of two or more corporations which, if certain criteria as to continuity are met, is treated for accounting purposes as if a new basis of accountability does not arise.

8. *Recommended presentation of prior years.* When comparative statements are presented, the AICPA recommends that the results of operations of the several constituent companies during periods prior to the year of combination should be stated on a combined basis or, if more informative, should be shown separately. Disclosure must also be made of the treatment of the business combination as a pooling of interests. But if the recommended presentation is followed, the standard reference to "on a basis consistent with that of the preceding year" or "on a consistent basis" may be used.

9. *Lack of consistency.* If comparative statements are not in conformity with the foregoing recommended method of presentation, an inconsistency arises, not because of any change in accounting principles in the current year but because the prior years' statements do not give the appropriate recognition to the pooling. In this circumstance, the opinion paragraph should state the inconsistency and refer to a note to the financial statements which describes the pooling and its effect on earnings of the prior years included in the report.

10. *Single-year statements.* When statements are presented only for the current year, the auditor may use the standard wording on consistency in the opinion paragraph providing there is a note to the financial statements adequately disclosing the pooling and stating the separate or combined net incomes of the constituent companies for the preceding year.

CHAPTER **5**

ACCOUNTING AND REPORTING
PROBLEMS AND APPLICATIONS

In Chapter 4 we dealt with reporting from the standpoint of basic concepts and standards. In this chapter we will concern ourselves with a number of selected accounting and reporting problems which are the subject of current professional concern. Some of these problems, such as accounting for price-level changes, are controversial whereas others, like the question of the proper preparation and use of the statement of source and application of funds, are designed to deal with misleading reporting practices. As a matter of comprehensiveness of coverage, this chapter will also include more traditional topics such as reporting principles for consolidated financial statements.

INCOME TAX ALLOCATION

The subject of income tax allocation and the accounting principles which pertain to it are discussed in ARB No. 43, Chapter 10, and in ARB No. 44 (Revised).

Question—November 1961 (7)

Many companies report taxable income which is different from their accounting income because generally accepted accounting principles are not always appropriate for determination of taxable income. When such differences occur, they raise a question as to whether the income tax amount shown in the income statement should be (1) the amount of taxes actually payable for the period or (2) the amount

143

which is allocable to (that is, the amount which would be payable on) the income reported in the income statement.

(a) Briefly discuss income tax allocation. Include in your discussion a definition of the term and the arguments for allocation.

(b) List six arguments which have been advanced against income tax allocation.

Solution

Income Tax Allocation

1. *Financial accounting versus tax accounting.* The question of income tax allocation arises because items of revenue or expense are treated differently for Federal income tax purposes as compared with financial accounting.

2. *Examples.* For tax purposes, for example, a company may use the declining-balance or other accelerated depreciation methods, but straight-line depreciation is used on the books (that is, for financial statement purposes). The installment basis of accounting may be used for tax purposes, but the full sales accrual basis of revenue determination is used for financial accounting purposes.

3. *Interperiod tax allocation.* The foregoing examples are illustrations of differences between books and tax return which carry over into future periods, and the allocation required is therefore referred to as *interperiod allocation.* Thus, in the depreciation example, depreciation is greater on the tax return in the earlier years but lower than the books in later years.

4. *Intraperiod tax allocation.* Tax and book differences are sometimes limited to a single year and entail what is referred to as *intraperiod allocation.* An example of this is the inclusion on the tax return as an income or expense item of an extraordinary gain or loss which is excluded from income and reflected in the statement of retained earnings for financial accounting purposes.

5. *Allocation procedure.* Income tax allocation is a procedure whereby a provision is made on the books for income tax expense based not on the income tax due but, rather, on the income reported for financial accounting purposes. In this way a proper matching is achieved of Federal income tax expense and income as shown on the financial statements. The difference between income tax expense as shown on the books and the actual tax liability for the years as shown on the income tax return is shown in the financial statements as follows: in an intraperiod allocation situation, in retained earnings as an offset against the extraordinary gain or loss reflected therein;

as a liability for deferred taxes for an interperiod allocation situation such as straight-line versus accelerated depreciation method; or as a deferred charge for an interperiod situation in which the earlier years show a higher taxable income than the comparable income per the books.

Arguments for Allocation

1. *Matching.* Tax allocation contributes to a better matching of income and expense by charging the tax to accounting periods in relation to reported net income rather than to the taxable income.

2. *Taxes as expense.* Federal income taxes is an expense and is allocable, in the same way as any other expense, to other accounts and accounting periods.

3. *Deferral versus saving.* Where the tax treatment results in a taxable income lower than reported income in the earlier period, this results not in an absolute tax saving but rather in a deferral of tax which will have to be paid in the later years when taxable income will be higher than book income.

4. *Existence of liability.* The deferral is in fact a liability which must be accrued in the same manner as expenses or other estimated liabilities.

5. *Reduction in asset value.* Deferred taxes may, alternatively, sometimes be considered asset valuation accounts designed to reflect a diminution in asset value. This comes about in a case in which, for example, accelerated depreciation on the tax return in an earlier period removes to that extent from the asset, as stated on the books, the tax-deductibility utility associated with a depreciable asset.

6. *Conservatism.* If a deferred tax liability were not created, income for the year could be considered to be overstated and the doctrine of conservatism disregarded.

7. *Going concern.* It is assumed that, on a going concern basis, the deferred taxes will in fact have to be paid in the future periods.

Arguments Against Allocation

1. *Absence of liability.* Deferred income taxes is not a liability. There is no debt to the government for taxes, nor is any being claimed.

2. *Uncertainty.* There is uncertainty both with respect to future tax rates and taxable income. The company, for example, may experience losses in future years thus nullifying any deferred tax liability.

3. *Permanent deferral.* Deferred taxes associated with accelerated depreciation and similar differences between tax and book income

may be deferred indefinitely as long as the level of investment in fixed assets continues. This may result in permanent balances or residuals in deferred tax accounts.

4. *Ultimate cancellation of differences.* Differences between taxable income and accounting income caused by timing may tend to cancel themselves out in future years. For example, at a point where depreciation on some units of equipment for tax purposes becomes lower than the corresponding book amount, tax depreciation on newer units of property will be higher than book depreciation, thereby canceling out any differences.

5. *Equalization of income.* Tax allocation involves a form of artificial income smoothing. The tax falling against the income of a period should simply be the tax liability for the period.

6. *Distribution of profits.* Federal income taxes are not really an expense, but can be viewed as a distribution after net income from operations has been determined. If it is not an expense, it is not allocable.

INVESTMENT TAX CREDIT

The Revenue Act of 1962 provided an investment tax credit for business amounting to a maximum of 7% of investments in tangible personal property in general if the useful life of the property is eight years or more. The credit is a direct reduction of the tax. The principles relating to the accounting for the investment credit are stated in APB Opinion No. 4, which amended APB Opinion No. 2.

Question—May 1965 (7)

The Revenue Act of 1962, amended by the Revenue Act of 1964, provides for an "investment tax credit." Two methods of accounting for investment credits are (1) reduction in a cost otherwise chargeable in a greater amount to future accounting periods, and (2) reduction in taxes otherwise applicable to the income of the year in which the credit arises. Periodic income may differ materially depending on which of the two accounting methods is selected.

(a) Describe the above two methods of accounting for the investment credit. What is the effect of each on periodic income determination?

(b) Present the arguments advanced for each method.

Solution

Description of Methods

1. *Cost reduction method.* This method is preferred by the APB. The tax credit is treated either as a reduction in asset cost or as deferred income. In either event it is amortized over the productive life of the acquired property. The amortization may therefore take the form of either reduced depreciation charges (the asset being depreciated on the basis of cost less the tax credit) or of periodic transfers to income from the deferred credit amount. Thus the effect of this method is to increase periodic income over the life of the acquired asset.

2. *Selective tax reduction.* This method is acceptable but not preferred. The tax credit is taken into income in full in the year granted and is treated as a reduction of the tax otherwise applicable to the year in which it arose.

Arguments for Cost Reduction Method

1. *Cost reduction.* The cost of acquiring fixed assets is measured by the necessary cash outlay. The investment tax credit is a specific reduction of the outlay by way of tax saving.

2. *Legislative intent.* The intention of the law is to stimulate investment in property by way of cost reduction.

3. *Income distortion.* The cost method eliminates the material impact of the tax credit upon income in a single year.

4. *Use of property.* Earnings stem from the use of property not from its acquisition; the credit should, therefore, be amortized over the life of the property acquired.

5. *Income realization.* Income is not considered to be realized at the time property is acquired. Hence, cost savings, bargain purchases, or taxes credits are not realized income.

6. *Recapture element.* There is uncertainty as to the amount of credit that will be retained because of the recapture provision of the law which provides for a repayment of the credit under certain circumstances. It is therefore more conservative not to take the full credit into income in the year it arises.

Arguments for Selective Tax Reduction

1. *Tax reduction.* The investment tax credit is in fact a selective tax reduction applicable in full to the year in which it arises.

2. *Overall earnings.* Whether any benefit is derived from the investment tax credit depends upon the overall earnings of the business.

Earnings cannot be attributed to the specific asset acquisition giving rise to the tax credit. Therefore, the tax benefit is not relevant to the specific asset and should not be amortized.

3. *Cost outlay.* The cost of an asset is the cash price paid to another entity and should not be affected by considerations involving parties not directly involved in the exchange transaction.

4. *Intention.* Although it was the government's intention to stimulate investment through the tax credit, only the entity's intention is important in choosing the proper accounting for its operations.

5. *Varying costs.* Under the cost reduction method, identical assets would be recorded by different companies at varying costs despite the same purchase prices, with the cost being dependent not entirely on the exchange transactions but also on the particular tax situation of each company.

6. *Gratuitous tax benefits.* The investment credit is really a gratuitous tax benefit because a company is entitled to it even though it purchases property in no greater quantities than it would in the absence of a tax credit.

PRICE-LEVEL ADJUSTMENTS

Generally accepted accounting principles dictate that financial statements be prepared on an historical cost basis without adjustment for any impact that price-level changes may have on the financial statements. What precisely is meant by the term *price-level adjustments?*

Question—November 1964 (7c)

In their discussion about accounting for changes in price levels and the methods of measuring them, uninformed individuals have frequently failed to distinguish between adjustments for changes in the price levels of specific goods and services, and adjustments for changes in the general purchasing power of the dollar. What is the distinction? Which are "price-level adjustments"? Discuss.

Solution

1. *General versus specific changes.* Adjustment for changes in the price level of specific goods and services is a form of replacement cost accounting, to be distinguished from price-level adjustments due to changes in the general purchasing power of the dollar.

2. *Specific goods.* The change in price of a specific commodity

may take place for reasons of supply and demand and other economic factors apart from changes in the general price level. Moreover, the trend of prices in general, which measures the stability of the dollar, may even run counter to the price change as reflected by a specific price index.

3. *Commodity index.* Adjustment for specific commodity price changes is accomplished by applying a specific commodity price index to the book value of an asset or by appraisal techniques.

4. *General index.* An index of general price-level changes (such as the Consumer Price Index, the Wholesale Price Index, or the Gross National Product Implicit Price Deflator) applied to historical cost values is designed to adjust for changes in the value of the dollar caused by economy-wide inflation or deflation.

5. *Common dollar.* Adjustment through an index of general purchasing power does not result in current values, but rather adjusts the financial statements expressed in historical dollars (that is, dollars of different purchasing power) to current or common dollars (that is, dollars reflecting current purchasing power).

6. *Illustration.* The distinction between the two adjustments may be illustrated with reference to a particular asset such as an office building. A specific price adjustment could be accomplished through the use of the American Appraisal Company index for nonresidential buildings. The Gross National Product Implicit Price Deflator would be used for "price-level adjustment" purposes to measure, in terms of purchasing power, the number of current dollars that equate to the dollar outlay at the time the asset was acquired.

PROS AND CONS OF PRICE-LEVEL ADJUSTMENTS

The arguments which have been advanced in favor of and against the adjustment of the general-purpose financial statements to reflect price-level changes constitute, in effect, a reexamination of basic accounting concepts.

Question—November 1964 (7a,b)

A common objective of accountants is to prepare meaningful financial statements. To attain this objective, many accountants maintain that the financial statements must be adjusted for changes in price level. Other accountants believe that financial statements should continue to be prepared on the basis of unadjusted historical cost.

List the arguments for adjusting financial statements for changes in price level. List the arguments for preparing financial statements only on the basis of unadjusted historical cost.

Solution

Arguments for Price-Level Adjustments

1. *Unstable dollar.* The dollar, which is the unit of measurement in accounting, is an unstable measure and dollars of different accounting periods are not comparable. Price-level adjustments are designed to restate financial statement data in terms of a common dollar, that is, a dollar representing its current purchasing power.

2. *Income determination.* Unadjusted income data do not properly reflect the earning power of a company. Revenues are generally stated in terms of current dollars; but costs, especially depreciation and amortization, are stated in terms of dollars of varying price levels. For example, the dollar spent to purchase machinery ten years ago may represent twice the value of the current dollar. Price-level adjusted income statements are therefore more realistic and clearly separate the real results of operations from mere inflationary effects on corporate income.

3. *Comparative statements.* The use of common dollars will make statements more comparable with respect to the comparative statements of a single company and of companies in a particular industry.

4. *Stewardship.* Price-level adjusted statements are more useful for evaluating management's stewardship.

5. *Management.* The failure to reflect price-level changes can result in an overstatement of income in terms of current dollars and lead to dividend, wage, expansion, and other management policies inconsistent with the real earnings.

6. *Income taxes.* The charging of low historical costs to revenues which are stated in more current dollars results in an overstatement of true earnings and, hence, in overpayment of income taxes.

7. *Economic data.* Corporate financial reports and statistics would be better suited for economic analysis necessary for establishing governmental fiscal policies, taxation, rate-making, etc.

Arguments for Historical Statements

1. *Objectivity.* Historical cost statements are based on the actual dollars involved in the original transaction and are therefore objective in nature.

2. *Cost principle.* Price-level adjustments require writing-up fixed assets and recording gains on long-term debt, thus violating both the cost principle and the realization principle.

3. *Supplementary statements.* The impact of inflation on financial data can be disclosed in supplementary statements.

4. *Values.* Unlike replacement cost or specific index number adjustments, a price-level adjusted balance sheet would not reflect the current values for specific assets.

5. *Legal aspects.* The dollar is not just a measuring unit but is legal tender and a medium of exchange. Its use as a stable unit in the business world in contractual transactions requires that it be so used in accounting.

6. *Familiarity.* Financial statements prepared in terms of historical dollars are familiar to, and accepted by, the reader. Adjusted statements would create confusion.

7. *Degree of inflation.* Price-level changes in the United States have been gradual and have not affected financial data based on historical cost sufficiently to warrant adjustment.

8. *Asset turnover.* The turnover of net current assets including inventory insures that these items are in effect stated at current costs. The growth of capital investment spurred by technological improvements and the growth in demand mean that a significant portion of fixed assets is also stated at approximately current cost.

9. *Effect on economy.* Price-level adjusted statements may have the effect of contributing to inflationary pressures through price increases based on higher costs.

10. *Taxation.* Price-level adjusted statements are not acceptable for tax purposes. Approval for this purpose as well as government sanction of the method in general are necessary for the general acceptance of price-level adjustments.

11. *Method of adjustment.* The selection of an appropriate index or the construction of an acceptable index which would be uniformly and universally applied is essential if comparability is to be maintained among companies. There is no generally accepted index and method for adjusting financial statements.

12. *Valuation methods.* Accelerated depreciation methods and Lifo inventory valuation method compensate to some extent for price-level increases by charging higher amounts to income.

DEPRECIATION AND HIGH COSTS

The following is a summary of ARB No. 43, Chapter 9A, which sets forth the AICPA position on accounting under conditions of inflation.

1. *The problem of replacement.* In view of the increases in the price level, management is faced with the problem of plant replacement at higher costs.

2. *Management policies.* In reflecting depreciation as a cost with respect to product pricing and similar policies, management must also consider that the cost of plant replacement increases with the price level.

3. *Surplus reserve.* As an aid to future replacement of facilities at higher prices, management can make annual appropriations of retained earnings.

4. *Improper depreciation charges.* The recording of depreciation on any other than on a cost basis and by the use of appropriate depreciation methods would violate generally accepted accounting principles.

5. *Examples of improper depreciation methods.* The following are examples of improper depreciation practices in this regard: depreciation on replacement cost; depreciation on appraised values; immediate write-downs of plant cost in amounts corresponding to inflated costs.

6. *Committee recommendations.* The committee on accounting procedure recommends the following:

(a) There should be no change in the accepted method of accounting for assets at cost.

(b) If inflation increases to the point where dollar costs lose their significance, it might then become necessary to restate all assets on an adjusted price-level basis.

7. *Supplementary statements.* The reason for the need to retain a greater portion of earnings for plant replacement, and hence the inability to increase dividend distributions, pay higher wages, or reduce prices, can be explained to interested persons in supplemental schedules or footnotes to the financial statements.

QUASI-REORGANIZATIONS

A restatement of assets in a quasi-reorganization is essentially the only circumstance in which departures from the historical cost basis of accounting are permitted. The procedures and disclosure requirements involved are discussed in ARB No. 43, Chapter 7, and ARB No. 46.

Question—May 1962 (4)

The president of Woodie Corporation, your client, has asked you for an explanation of a "quasi-reorganization." He is unfamiliar with

the procedure and is concerned that a competitor might have an advantage since undergoing a "quasi-reorganization."
Prepare a report for the president explaining the "quasi-reorganization." Your report should include the following points:

1. Definition and accounting features of the procedure.
2. The purpose of the procedure. Under what conditions should it be considered?
3. Authorization necessary.
4. Disclosure required in the financial statements.
5. Does the competitor have an advantage? Discuss briefly.

Solution

1. *Definition and accounting features.* A quasi-reorganization is an accounting procedure involving the restatement of accounts on substantially the same basis as if a new company were being established. Thus deficits would be eliminated, assets would be restated at current values, and the capital accounts would reflect the new capitalization for stockholder equities. The legal entity itself, as well as the corporate debt, would remain unchanged.

Assets should be written down to realistic values so as not to burden future income with charges for overstated assets. However, assets should not be written down below realizable values or fair values and so result in overstating the earnings of future periods. Provision should also be made for known losses or expenses incurred prior to the date of the quasi-reorganization.

All charges for losses and asset write-downs should first be made against retained earnings. The resulting deficit, if any, should then be charged against paid in surplus. The par value of capital stock may be reduced, where necessary, to create a paid in surplus for the absorption of a deficit.

2. *Purpose of procedure.* The purpose of a quasi-reorganization is to give the corporation a fresh start, "as-if" it were a new corporation. Future operations are unburdened by losses embodied in overstated assets. The stigma associated with an accumulated deficit on the balance sheet is erased and the corporation may begin anew to accumulate earnings and to pay dividends.

3. *Authorization.* The nature and extent of authorization necessary depend upon the laws of the state in which the corporation is organized. In general, the formal approval of the stockholders should be obtained.

4. *Disclosure.* Full disclosure of the quasi-reorganization should

be made in footnotes to the financial statements. Retained earnings on future balance sheets should be dated so as to disclose to the reader the new date from which the earnings have been accumulated. This dating of retained earnings would rarely be required after a 10-year period following the readjustment and often can be dispensed with earlier.

5. *Competitive advantage.* The quasi-reorganization in and of itself does not improve the competitive ability of a company. It merely enables a company to prepare more realistic financial statements following the readjustment. The factors affecting competition are unchanged. The adjusted cost data, however, would provide management with more useful information for pricing and other business decisions.

NATURAL BUSINESS YEAR

The desirability of the use of the natural business year as a basis for financial reporting has been emphasized by the SEC in Accounting Series Releases Nos. 17 and 19 and by the AICPA in a number of its publications. The natural business year yields many advantages with respect to both the planning of an audit engagement and the reliability of the financial statements.

The natural business year of a company is the one wherein the annual cycle of its activity ends when its inventories, receivables, liabilities, loans from banks, and its business activities are at their lowest point. The year may end on December 31 (calendar-year closing) or at another month-end (fiscal-year closing). It would be determined by preparation of a schedule showing monthly balances (preferably for a number of years) and percentage of each month's balance to the total for a 12-month period for the following: production; inventories (by classification); sales; accounts receivable; accounts payable; and notes payable.

Question—November 1955 (6)

You have been engaged as the independent accountant for a new corporation engaged in manufacturing, and have been asked to advise whether the corporation should prepare its financial reports on a calendar-year basis or use a fiscal year corresponding to its "natural business year."

State fully the usual advantages to the client and to the auditor of using a natural business year instead of a calendar year.

Solution

1. When the natural year is other than a calendar year, the auditor can render more effective services because of avoidance of tax-season pressures and staff shortages.

2. The auditor can spread much of his work throughout the year.

3. The employment of temporary employees during a short peak seasonal period will be avoided and thus obviate the reliance upon such staff accountants who have not been adequately trained in the CPA firm's methods.

4. The income statement will be based on a natural and completed cycle of business operations rather than on an artificial period.

5. A review of the propriety and soundness of the accounting principles and methods will be facilitated because incomplete transactions would be at a minimum. Transactions which straddle two accounting periods raise complex problems with respect to the recognition of revenue and cost allocations.

6. Because inventories and receivables are at their low point, fewer problems exist with respect to inventory pricing and valuation and estimates of bad debt losses. Similarly, fewer accruals and adjustments for prepayments and deferred costs are necessary.

7. The balance sheet will show the most liquid position—a considerable aid for the client in obtaining credit.

8. Because of the reduced amounts involved there is less likelihood of income tax disputes relating to inventory valuation, bad-debts allowance, and other items involving estimates and judgments.

FOREIGN EXCHANGE

The basis for translating assets, liabilities, losses, and gains into dollars from foreign currencies in consolidating or combining accounts with foreign branches is set forth in ARB No. 43, Chapter 12.

Question—May 1955 (8a,b)

The ABC Manufacturing Corporation during the current year opened a manufacturing and selling branch in X country. At the year-end the official rate of currency exchange with country X was

12 to $1 and the unofficial free-market rate was 15 to $1. In combining the statements of the branch with those of the parent at year-end, at what value would the following branch accounts be reflected in the combined balance sheet—accounts receivable, fixed assets, inventories, short-term debt, and long-term debt?

How is the gain or loss resulting from the translation of the foreign currency into U.S. currency reflected in the balance sheet of ABC Corporation at year-end?

Solution

1. *Different rates.* The point is made in ARB No. 43, Chapter 12, that if more than one exchange rate exists, selection should be made of the one that is the most realistic and appropriate. The official rate should be selected because its use would be more conservative and more consistent with legitimate business practices.

2. *Accounts receivable.* Unless covered by forward exchange contracts, current assets including cash and accounts receivable should be translated at the exchange rate quoted as of the balance sheet date. Long-term receivables can be translated at the exchange rates which prevailed at their inception, but it is stated in APB Opinion No. 6 that a translation at current exchange rates is appropriate in many circumstances.

3. *Fixed assets.* These assets should be translated into dollars at the exchange rates which existed at the time of acquisition or construction. If items were paid for in United States dollars, that dollar cost would be used. In the event the assets were acquired shortly before a substantial and permanent change in the exchange rate, that new rate might be more appropriately used in the translation.

4. *Inventories.* The general rule is that inventories are translated on the same basis as current assets generally, namely, at the rate prevailing at the balance sheet date. In applying the usual rule of the lower of cost or market, however, consideration should be given to the possibility that the inventories might be currently replaceable at a higher amount than cost, both being initially expressed in foreign currency. It would then not be appropriate to reflect cost routinely at the current lower exchange rate because the higher replacement cost would, in effect, compensate for the lower exchange rate.

5. *Debt.* Current liabilities are translated at the exchange rates quoted on the balance sheet date. Long-term liabilities (and capital stock) are usually stated at the exchange rates prevailing at the time they were originally incurred; but according to APB Opinion No.

6, long-term liabilities can appropriately in many circumstances be stated at current exchange rates.

6. *Gain or loss.* Realized losses or gains on foreign exchange should be reflected in income. If exchange losses, however, are so material because of unprecedented developments that their inclusion in income would make the income statement misleading, they should be charged to retained earnings. Unrealized losses resulting from declines in translation values should be provided for by a charge to income. Unrealized gains, however, should be carried in a suspense account, except to the extent that they can be used to offset prior provisions for unrealized losses.

CONSOLIDATED STATEMENTS

Consolidated statements usually provide a more meaningful presentation than separate statements, but there are limitations to the usefulness of such statements.

Question—May 1960 (6)

The use of consolidated financial statements has become a common practice in published financial reports of American corporations. However, consolidated reports do not serve all of the purposes for which individual statements may be used. List and briefly discuss five limitations of the usefulness of consolidated reports.

Solution

1. *Information.* Consolidated financial statements show the financial position and results of operations of the consolidated entity taken as a whole. Thus information regarding the position or profitability of individual companies which may be desired by the individual companies' creditors, minority stockholders, or potential investors is unavailable.

2. *Legal entity.* The consolidated statements do not present the data regarding a legal entity. Each subsidiary is a separate legal entity with its own creditors having claims against the subsidiaries' assets. Consolidated assets are not available to creditors of individual subsidiaries, and consolidated working capital does not carry the usual significance of this measure.

3. *Individual operations.* Operating results of individual com-

panies are obscured. Losses sustained by some subsidiaries are offset by profits of other companies in the consolidated group. Similarly, a weak financial position of one company is offset by a strong position of another company.

4. *Dividends.* Consolidated retained earnings is not necessarily an indication of the amount available for dividends; indeed, the consolidated entity does not declare or pay dividends.

5. *Comparability.* Consolidated statements of heterogeneous operations make difficult comparative analysis of results with other companies or with industry statistics.

6. *Ratio analyses.* Ratio analyses which depend upon relationships between balance sheet and income statement values of an entity are less significant because of the averaging of such values resulting from consolidation.

EXCLUSION OF SUBSIDIARIES FROM CONSOLIDATED REPORTS

Under certain circumstances fair presentation requires that subsidiaries be excluded from consolidated reports.

Question—November 1964 (4a)

The use of consolidated financial statements for reporting to stockholders is common. Under some conditions, however, it is desirable to exclude a subsidiary from consolidated reports. List the conditions under which a subsidiary should be excluded from consolidated statements.

Solution

1. *Control.* The parent company must have a controlling interest in the subsidiaries. Financial control is evidenced by the ownership directly or indirectly of over 50% of the voting shares of another corporation. Control must be continuing and not temporary.

2. *Large minority interest.* The size of the minority interest in relation to the equity of the parent in the consolidated net assets may be material enough to call for the preparation of unconsolidated statements.

3. *Unrelated activity.* The fact that related companies are heterogeneous in nature of activity is not in itself a criterion for exclusion.

However, there are situations where separate statements may be required for subsidiaries in special industries like banking, insurance, and financing.

4. *Foreign subsidiaries.* Foreign subsidiaries whose assets are in jeopardy, or where currency is blocked, should not be consolidated.

INTERCOMPANY PROFITS

Consolidated statements are presentations of a single business entity. Hence, all intercompany accounts and intercompany transactions must be eliminated. ARB No. 51 points out that intercompany profits and losses on assets still within the possession of a member of the consolidated group should be eliminated and that the basis for elimination is generally gross profit or loss.

Question—November 1964 (4b)

The existence of intercompany profits in consolidated inventories as a result of sales by a less than wholly owned subsidiary to its parent has given rise to the following three viewpoints as to how such profits should be treated when preparing consolidated financial statements.

1. Only the parent company's share of intercompany profits in inventory should be eliminated.

2. The entire amount of intercompany profits in inventory should be eliminated against the equities of the controlling and minority groups in proportion to their interests.

3. The entire amount of intercompany profits in inventories should be eliminated against consolidated retained earnings.

Give arguments that are used to support each treatment. Discuss the theoretical propriety or impropriety, as the case may be, of each treatment.

Solution

It can be argued that the elimination of only the parent's share of intercompany profits in inventory is justified on the ground that the minority interest's share of this profit has been realized. The theory is that consolidated statements are designed to portray the interests of the parent company and not of the minority. No recognition is given to the fact that the parent company directs all of the activities of the subsidiary and thereby is in complete control of the subsidiaries' assets.

The full elimination of intercompany profits conforms to generally accepted accounting principles and to the idea that the consolidated statements represent a single business enterprise. The elimination may be charged to the controlling interest and to the minority interest in accordance with their relative interests. Under this approach minority interests are not considered outside interests or "quasi-legal" creditors, but rather are viewed as an element of proprietorship in consolidated net assets. The allocation of a portion of the elimination to the minority interest is necessary for fair presentation of their equity in the consolidated net assets as well as the equity of the controlling group.

The elimination of intercompany profits against consolidated retained earnings is another acceptable way of comforming with the requirement that the full intercompany profit be eliminated. In this instance, however, the parent company's interest is viewed as being a 100% interest corresponding to the parent's total economic control.

BUSINESS COMBINATIONS—PURCHASE VERSUS POOLING

APB Opinion No. 6 states that the criteria set forth in ARB No. 48 for distinguishing between a purchase and a pooling of interests are to be used as guides rather than as requirements and that the bulletin be considered as an overall expression of philosophy rather than a statement of principles.

Question—November 1960 (6a)

The terms *purchase* and *pooling of interests* describe two methods designating the result of bringing together two or more corporations into a combination for the purpose of carrying on the previously conducted business. Define the terms *purchase* and *pooling of interests* as used to designate business combinations.

Solution

A pooling of interests arises where substantially all of the ownership interests of the combining corporations continue as owners of either the surviving company or of a new company that is formed to take over the assets and liabilities of the combining companies. The continuance of one of the companies as a subsidiary does not prevent the transaction from being a pooling.

A business combination is considered to be a purchase when a substantial part of the ownership interests of the corporation being acquired is eliminated or where other factors tending to establish a pooling of interests, as set forth below, are not present. The distinction between a purchase and a pooling of interests rests on the substance of the transaction and the surrounding circumstances rather than on the legal form or on the tax consequences.

The following are some considerations relating to ownership and other factors which tend to indicate that the business combination should be treated as a pooling of interests rather than a purchase.

1. *New shares.* The distribution of new shares to the owners of an acquired company is such that their new interest is substantially proportional to their former interest.

2. *Voting.* The relative voting rights of the combining corporation should not be significantly modified through the use of nonvoting stock or senior obligations.

3. *Retirement.* There should be no plan or intention to retire the ownership interest acquired by the former owners of a constituent company.

4. *Operations.* There should be a continuity of operations of the constituents. Sale or abandonment of a constituent may be considered a sign of a purchase.

5. *Management.* There should be a continuity of the managements of the constituents. This covers the power to control management as well. Where the management of a constituent has limited influence on the overall management of the enterprise, this may be indicative of a purchase.

6. *Relative size.* When one of the constituents is substantially dominant, a purchase rather than pooling may be presumed, but relative size is not necessarily a crucial factor.

7. *Overall appraisal.* No single factor is determinative of whether a combination is a pooling or a purchase. Rather, it is all factors, combined and cumulative, that are to be considered.

PURCHASE VERSUS POOLING—ACCOUNTING TREATMENT

A considerable difference in accounting treatment will result from a decision to classify a business combination as a purchase or a pooling of interests.

Question—November 1960 (6b)

Describe the accounting treatment for a purchase and for a pooling of interests.

Solution

Assets acquired in a combination deemed to be a purchase are accounted for at cost. Where consideration other than cash is given, the value assigned to the assets is based on the fair value of the consideration given or the fair value of the consideration received, whichever is more readily determinable and clearly evident. These principles correspond to those customarily applicable in the usual purchase of assets.

In a business combination deemed to be a pooling of interests, the book values of the assets of the constituent corporations as well as their surpluses and deficits are carried over and combined; thus a new accounting basis does not arise.

The consequences of the two methods of accounting may be illustrated by reference to depreciation and to dividends. Thus, if the current values of assets acquired in a business combination are higher than the book value of those assets, annual depreciation would be higher (and net income lower) if the combination were treated as a purchase. (Periodic amortization of goodwill—recorded in the event of a purchase—would have similar consequences.) But in a pooling of interests, the combined retained earnings would be higher than if the combination were treated as a purchase, and hence a more liberal dividend policy might be adopted.

The continuation of an acquired company in a pooling does not preclude the combining of retained earnings balances in consolidation. It is also to be noted that where a single corporation emerges from a purchase. (Periodic amortization of goodwill—recorded in the event stated capitals of the constituent corporations. In the former case, the excess may be deducted from any other paid in surplus first before being applied to retained earnings. In the latter case, the excess of the constituents' stated capital over the survivor's stated capital becomes part of the paid in surplus of the survivor.

LONG-TERM LEASES

ARB Opinion No. 5 takes the position that leases which are in substance installment purchases of property should be treated as the purchase of fixed assets with a corresponding recording of the liability, probably at the discounted amount of payments under the lease. Some accountants believe that all long-term leases, whether or not they are purchases in substance, are essentially financing arrangements which entail the acquisition by the lessee of an asset in the form of a property right and a corresponding obligation to the lessor, both being computed at the present value of future rental payments. APB Opinion No. 5 expresses the opinion, however, that such leases are simply executory contracts which do not create assets and liabilities of the type described.

Question—November 1961 (3a)

To keep funds free for working capital purposes, many companies prefer to rent facilities under a long-term lease with a renewal option rather than purchase them. In such cases it has been suggested that the value of the leasehold be displayed as an asset in the tenant's balance sheet and that a liability be established for the obligation incurred.

List and discuss briefly the arguments for and against recording the leasehold and the liability on the tenant's books.

Solution

For Capitalization

1. *Financing arrangement.* Leasing is merely an alternative form of financing the purchase of property and therefore should be accounted for as an installment purchase. The financing element is most clearly evident in a sale and leaseback arrangement.

2. *Acquisition of asset.* The right to use property under a lease for a long-term period is as much an asset of a business as property owned outright; it is the use of assets that produces income. Moreover, the property right is no less an asset because payment is "deferred" in the form of periodic rental payments.

3. *Liabilities.* On a going concern basis, the present value of the future lease rentals is a liability of the company which should be disclosed on the balance sheet. Footnote disclosure does not reveal the full liability nor place it within the proper context in the financial statements.

4. *Comparability.* Lease capitalization would provide a more meaningful basis for determining the return on investment of a com-

pany as well as facilitate comparative analysis with other companies which actually purchase rather than lease assets.

Against Capitalization

1. *Ownership.* Leased assets are not owned by the business and hence are not its assets.

2. *Absence of liability.* In the absence of the receipt of a valid asset, it would be improper to record a liability. The lease is an executory contract and there is no present liability for future rentals. Rentals are due each period for the use of the property for that specific period. Even in bankruptcy the court recognizes only three years' rental as an obligation.

3. *Method of computation.* The computation of the value of the asset entails certain difficulties with respect to the interest factor to be used in discounting rentals, and the elimination of maintenance, taxes, etc., to the extent they may have been included in rentals.

4. *Effect on borrowing.* Contractual agreements which limit borrowing or require that all fixed assets purchased be subject to an existing mortgage, might be jeopardized if leases are recorded as assets and liabilities.

5. *Taxes.* State and local taxes levied on property might be applied to leased assets if capitalized.

6. *Legal form.* Capitalization is a repudiation of the legal form of the transaction which management has selected and defeats the advantages of the lease form.

7. *Disclosure.* Adequate disclosure of lease obligations can be made in footnotes to financial statements.

CRITERIA FOR LEASE CAPITALIZATION

The following criteria are suggested in APB Opinion No. 5 for determining whether a lease agreement is fundamentally an installment purchase of property and, hence, should be capitalized; but it must be noted that the overall circumstances and combination of factors rather than a single criterion will be determinative.

1. *Equity.* A material equity in the property is created by the lease.

2. *Cancellability.* The lease is essentially noncancellable except on the ground of some remote contingency.

3. *Lease term.* An equity interest would be created if the initial

term of the lease is considerably less than the useful life of the property and the lessee has the option to renew the lease for the remaining period of the useful life of the property at less than fair rental.

4. *Purchase of property.* An equity interest is similarly created if the lessee is given the right to acquire the property, during or at the end of the lease, at a price considerably less than the probable fair value of the property.

5. *Special use.* A further indication that the arrangement is a purchase would exist if the property was acquired to meet the special needs of the lessee and can probably be used only for that purpose.

6. *Life of property.* The lease term corresponds to the estimated useful life of the property.

7. *Property expenses.* The lessee is required to pay such property expenses as taxes, insurance, and maintenance.

8. *Guarantees.* The lessee has undertaken to guarantee obligations of the lessor relating to the leased property.

9. *Tax treatment.* The lessee, for tax purposes, has treated the lease as a purchase.

10. *Related parties.* If the lessor and lessee are related parties, leases might be treated as purchases even in the absence of an equity build-up by the lessee under the following circumstances, providing the primary purpose of the lessor's ownership is to lease the property to the lessee:

(a) The rental payments are pledged to secure the lessor's debts.

(b) The lessee can control the lessor's actions with respect to the lease.

11. *Sale and leaseback.* Sale and leaseback arrangements often contain elements which suggest that a sale has not in fact taken place and that the original owner continues as the owner of the property in substance, necessitating a capitalization of the lease.

DISCLOSURE OF LONG-TERM LEASES

The disclosure requirements for lessees with respect to long-term leases are expressed in ARB No. 43, Chapter 14, and reaffirmed substantially in APB No. 5. The following is a summary of the latter's disclosure requirements.

1. *Commitments.* For leases which are not capitalized, the statements should disclose sufficient information to enable the reader to evaluate the effect of the lease commitments.

2. *Rentals.* Thus the notes to financial statements should disclose minimum annual rentals and the period of the leases.

3. *Additional disclosure.* The following are additional items that should usually be disclosed: types of property leased; obligations or guarantees; restrictions in agreements regarding dividends, debt, etc.; significant differences between minimum rentals and current year rentals.

4. *Manner of disclosure.* The details to be disclosed will vary with the circumstances. Thus rentals can be scheduled by periods of years; or the basis for calculating rent may be disclosed if determined by factors other than time.

5. *Sale and leaseback.* The principal details of such arrangements should be disclosed in the original year.

ACCOUNTING FOR LEASES IN FINANCIAL STATEMENTS OF LESSORS

The following is a summary of the views of the Accounting Principles Board on the lessor's accounting for leases as expressed in APB Opinion No. 7.

1. *Distinction in methods.* Fundamental to the discussion is the distinction which must be drawn between the "financing method" or the "operating method" used in allocating rentals and expenses to appropriate accounting periods covered by the lease.

2. *Financing method.* When the financing method is employed, the aggregate rentals are recorded as receivables and classified as current or noncurrent assets in accordance with the usual rules. These rentals are reduced by the amount of unearned interest which represents the excess of the aggregate rentals over the cost of the leased property (reduced by the estimated residual value as of the lease termination date). The unearned interest is then taken into income over the term of the lease, interest earned being computed in the usual financing manner based upon the declining balance of the unrecovered investment. Although the cost of the leased property will have been eliminated in the initial recording of the aggregate rentals, the residual value referred to above is classified separately in the fixed assets section of the balance sheet.

3. *Appropriateness of financing method.* The financing method should be used by lease-finance companies, banks, and similar institutions engaged in financing, and by manufacturers and others if the lease arrangement represents primarily a method of investing funds.

4. *Operating method.* Under the operating method leases are accounted for in the traditional manner, that is, rentals are recorded as revenues over the period of the lease, while the expenses of the leased property are depreciation, maintenance, and the other usua‍ costs.

5. *Appropriateness of operating method.* The operating method should be used if the lease arrangements are an integral part of the manufacturing operations or other operations of a business which are not basically of a financing nature.

6. *Leasing by manufacturers.* If certain conditions are met, manufacturers who lease their products should report the transaction as though it were an outright sale of merchandise, the revenue being stated at the lower of the amount that would have been received in a regular sale or the discounted amount of future rentals. The financing method would then be used to account for the rentals due, and the recorded sales value of the property would be treated as the "cost of leased property" as referred to in the financing method. The conditions which must be met to warrant recording the lease arrangement as a sale in effect are: credit risks must be determinable; the lessor does not retain major risks of ownership; and there are no material uncertainties regarding future costs or revenues under the lease. If any of these conditions are not met manufacturing profits should be recognized only as realized in the form of rental income.

7. *Disclosure.* The principal accounting methods used in accounting for leases should be disclosed in the financial statements.

INCOME AND RETAINED EARNINGS

The subject of the proper treatment of extraordinary items of profit or loss is discussed in ARB No. 43, Chapter 8. The advantages of the combined statement of income and retained earnings are set forth in ARB No. 43, Chapter 2.

Question—November 1961 (6a,b)

Information concerning the operations of a corporation may be presented in an income statement or in a combined "statement of income and retained earnings." Income statements may be prepared on a "current operating performance" basis ("earning power concept") or on an "all-inclusive" basis ("historical concept"). Proponents of the two types of income statements do not agree upon the proper treatment of material extraordinary charges and credits.

Define "current operating performance" and "all-inclusive" as used above.

Give the principal arguments for the use of each of the three statements: "all-inclusive" income statement, "current operating performance" income statement, and combined "statement of income and retained earnings."

Solution

Definition

The all-inclusive approach to the presentation of extraordinary items of profit and loss would reflect all such items, regardless of materiality, in the statement of income to be added or deducted in arriving at the final figure of net income. This concept is sometimes referred to as the clean-surplus theory because of the exclusion of such items from the statement of retained earnings.

The current operating performance concept would exclude extraordinary items from income and present them directly as charges or credits in the statement of retained earnings, thereby achieving a final net income figure on the statement of income which purports to represent the current results from the usual or typical operations of the period.

All-Inclusive

The principal arguments for the all-inclusive type of income statement are as follows:

1. *Life of enterprise.* When the net income figures for all past income statements are added together, the sum should represent the cumulative net income. This would not be possible under the current operating approach. The operating results for any one year are only tentative in nature and based essentially on estimates.

2. *Concept of net income.* Net income should be viewed according to a proprietary concept which regards net income as being determined by all factors which increase capital except, of course, dividends and capital transactions.

3. *Concealment.* The exclusion of the items in question from income may be looked upon as a concealment of significant elements of profit and loss. Their inclusion in the statement of retained earnings could be overlooked by the reader.

4. *Trends.* Extraordinary items can be significant factors in judging operating trends.

5. *Charges versus credits.* Over a period of years, charges involving extraordinary items tend to exceed the credits and the omission of all such items may in effect result in overstatements of net income.

6. *Manipulation.* The all-inclusive requirement precludes any manipulation based upon a determination as to whether or not an item is sufficiently material to exclude from net income, or whether or not an item is extraordinary in the first instance.

7. *Recurring versus nonrecurring.* It is frequently difficult to distinguish between recurring and nonrecurring items. Many so-called nonrecurring items do recur.

8. *Disclosure.* Although extraordinary items are included in the statement of income, they are nevertheless classified under a separate caption disclosing their nature.

Current Operating Performance

The following are the arguments often advanced in favor of the current operating performance concept.

1. *Concept of net income.* This school views the net income figure as one which indicates what a company was able to earn under the conditions prevailing in the period covered by the statement. The income should show the results from operations which are normal, usual, and typical and related only to the current year.

2. *Investor interest.* It is believed that the investor is interested in a single figure of net income as an index of how the company is likely to perform in the future. Hence, extraordinary items should be excluded because they are nonrecurring items.

3. *Professional judgment.* Management and the independent accountants are better able than the investor to decide whether extraordinary items may give rise to misleading inferences as to earnings potential and, therefore, should be excluded from income.

4. *Trends.* The proponents of the current operating performance concept do caution that it is risky to rely too heavily upon a single figure of net income and believe that trends over the years provide a better guide.

5. *Comparisons.* By excluding nonrecurring items, greater comparability is achieved in terms of both interperiod and intercompany comparisons.

Combined Statement of Income and Retained Earnings

The arguments for the combined statement are as follows:

1. *Significance of net income.* There can be a tendency to overstress the importance of net income for a single year. That figure

represents simply one installment in the earnings history of a company. The combined statement emphasizes this point of view.

2. *Extraordinary items.* When extraordinary items are reflected directly in the statement of retained earnings under the current operating performance concept, the combined statement more explicitly calls attention to such items and to their relationship to net income.

3. *Disclosure.* Unless the two statements are so intimately connected, the items excluded from net income can be overlooked and not given the proper consideration in any evaluation of the company's long-term capacity.

4. *Possible disadvantages.* Sometimes cited as disadvantages of the combined statement are: (a) the possibility that the reader may not see clearly the figure of net income which may be confused with the ending balance of retained earnings; and (b) the failure to sufficiently distinguish items that should be excluded from net income in the mistaken belief that the combined statement makes such refined distinctions unnecessary.

PRESENTATION OF EXTRAORDINARY ITEMS

The following discussion will serve to summarize the position of the AICPA on the presentation of extraordinary items of profit and loss.

Question—November 1961 (6b)

Explain the differences in content and organization of a "current operating performance" income statement and an "all-inclusive" income statement. Include a discussion of the proper treatment of material extraordinary charges and credits.

Solution

1. *All-inclusive concept.* As the name implies, this concept would reflect all material extraordinary items of profit and loss in a separate section of the statement of income following the caption "Net operating income" and before deducting Federal income taxes.

2. *Current operating performance concept—AICPA position.* The AICPA takes the position that there is to be a general presumption that all items of profit and loss are to be used in arriving at the final net income figure. However, items that are in the aggregate material and are not identifiable with the usual or typical opera-

tions of the period, should be excluded from net income if their inclusion would so impair the significance of net income that misleading inferences might be drawn. This exception to the foregoing general presumption would seem to tie the AICPA to the current operating performance school of thought.

3. *Examples of excluded items.* The following are five examples of types of items to be excluded:

(a) Material items related to prior years, such as income tax adjustments for prior years.

(b) Material gains and losses from unusual sales of assets not acquired for resale, such as fixed assets.

(c) Material losses like those from fire, earthquakes, and similar catastrophies.

(d) The lump-sum write-off of material amounts of intangibles.

(e) The write-off of the balance of unamortized bond discount or premium on the retirement or refunding of a debt.

4. *Capital items.* Any charges or credits relating to a company's own capital stock or to surplus appropriations must in any event be excluded from the determination of net income.

5. *Direct surplus presentation.* The preferable method of handling items of profit and loss excluded from the determination of net income is to show them directly in the statement of retained earnings, with full disclosure of their nature and amount. In the event that a combined statement of income and retained earnings is used, it is desirable that the figure of net income be followed immediately by the balance of retained earnings as of the beginning of the period.

6. *"Net income and special items."* A second method of handling extraordinary items under the current operating performance concept, which is also acceptable to the AICPA, is to present them in the income statement but following the figure designated as net income. This is the only method permitted by the S.E.C. When this approach is used, the final figure of net income must be clearly designated as such, while the caption following the addition or subtraction of the special items must be referred to by a term such as "net income and special items" so that the reader has no doubts about which figure represents the net income for the period. It is also understood that the special items which follow the figure of net income are to be regarded as direct debits or credits to retained earnings.

7. *Reporting of earnings per share.* Because of the major significance which the investor attaches to the single figure of net income or net income per share, it is important that when earnings are reported in newspapers, services, and the like, the per share amount of special items excluded from income be similarly reported.

EARNINGS PER SHARE

The methods of computing earnings per share are discussed in ARB No. 49. The method of computing earnings per share in the event of a change in the number of shares outstanding will depend on whether cash or other property has been received or paid. If there has been a stock dividend or stock split, the number of shares outstanding at the end of the year will be used in determining the earnings per share. However, if cash or property is involved in any increase or decrease during the year in the number of shares outstanding, then the computation of earnings per share must be made on a weighted average basis. The reason for this distinction is that in the case of the stock dividend or the stock split no changes in assets were involved, whereas in the other circumstance, the inflow or outflow of funds or property during the year and the corresponding impact on income (indirect, to be sure) require that the number of shares used in the computation be similarly adjusted.

In issuing earnings per share figures for comparative statements, a similar distinction is made. If changes in stock resulted from stock splits or stock dividends, it is necessary to adjust the number of shares outstanding in the years prior to the change, simply for computational purposes. No such restatement is necessary where capital stock changes involve cash or property on the ground that such asset changes, it is assumed, influenced the subsequent earnings.

SOURCE AND APPLICATION OF FUNDS

The position of the AICPA on the proper use and method of preparation of the statement of source and application of funds is expressed in APB Opinion No. 3 and summarized below.

1. *Definition.* In the broader sense, a statement of source and application of funds accounts for the change in working capital during a given period by presenting the factors which created the increases and decreases in working capital. The most common concept of "funds" has identified it with working capital. But it can also be used to represent cash itself. The statement, in that event, is often referred to as a cash flow statement. However, the term "cash flow" has been used more recently to mean the funds derived from operations. When used in that sense, cash flow would represent the net

income before deducting depreciation, depletion, amortization, and similar charges to income which did not require the use of funds during the period.

2. *Cash earnings.* When cash flow is used to denote the funds derived from operations, synonyms used to describe this include "cash earnings," "cash income," and "cash throw-off."

3. *Erroneous impressions.* When the term "cash earnings" or other synonyms are used for reporting purposes, it is possible for the reader to gain the erroneous impression that that designation is superior to net income as a measure of earning power. Similarly, price-cash flow ratios are sometimes substituted for price-earnings ratios for investment analysis purposes, and "cash flow per share" is often included in annual reports. Because of this emphasis on a figure of net income plus depreciation and similar noncash charges, the impression is being created that "cash earnings" represents a more meaningful index of earning capacity and of amounts available for dividend payments than does the figure of net income. Thus a company may have a loss and even a deficit despite a substantial cash flow and be unable to pay dividends, embark upon an expansion program, or engage in other activities seemingly consistent with the cash flow.

4. *Significance of net income.* It is the APB's opinion that the amount of funds derived from operations is in no way a substitute for the figure of net income as a measure of operating results. "Cash flow" and similar terms should not be used in annual reports in a way that would reflect upon the significance of net income. It is misleading to issue figures of "cash flow per share" because they downgrade the significant item of "earnings per share" and ignore plant replacement and other expenditures which have a counter impact on cash.

5. *Supplementary information.* The APB believes that a statement of source and application of funds is desirable as supplementary information but that its inclusion in the report is not mandatory. The APB does not cite the various uses to which the funds statement may be put, but the funds statement may be used to provide a more comprehensive picture of the factors which caused increases and decreases in working capital; to show the sources of funds (for example, operations, creditors, investors); and to disclose the disposition of funds (for example, dividends, plant acquisitions, and debt retirements). These data are extremely useful for interperiod and intercompany comparisons when reported for a period of years.

6. *Concept of funds.* The concept of "funds" should be related to the purpose of the statement, but when included in annual reports

the term should embrace all financial resources including non-working capital acquisitions of property (e.g., through issuance of securities).

ACCOUNTING FOR COSTS OF PENSION PLANS

Because the cost of most pension plans is material, the very fact that a plan has been adopted or an important amendment added should be disclosed in the financial statements in the year of occurrence. The disclosure requirements and the principles relating to the accounting for pension plans are set forth in APB Opinion No. 8 entitled "Accounting for the Cost of Pension Plans." The following are items that should be disclosed: existence of the plan and groups covered; accounting and funding methods employed; pension cost provision for the period; the excess, if any, of vested benefits (actuarially computed) over the total of the pension fund and any balance sheet pension accruals; and any factors, such as a change in accounting method, affecting the comparability of financial statements for the periods presented.

Question—November 1958 (7b)

The term *pension plan* has been referred to as a formal arrangement for employee retirement benefits, whether established unilaterally or through negotiation, by which commitments, specific or implied, have been made which can be used as the basis for estimating costs. What is the preferable procedure for computing and accruing the costs under a pension plan? Explain.

Solution

1. *Charges to income.* The costs of a pension plan should be periodically charged to income of the applicable accounting periods subsequent to the adoption or amendment of a plan. Such costs should never be charged to retained earnings, thus bypassing the income statement. This principle also applies to *past service costs* based on the past services of employees as determined at the inception of the plan, and also to *prior service costs* based on services of employees prior to a particular actuarial valuation date. These costs too were incurred for the benefit of current and future periods and should not therefore be charged against retained earnings.

2. *Relationships to amount funded.* The provision for pension cost does not necessarily have to be the same as the amount funded. Funding is essentially a financial management matter.

3. *Going concern.* A company's legal liability for pension costs may be limited by a provision that pensions are payable only out of the assets in the pension fund. Despite any such provisions, however, and unless there is convincing evidence that benefits set forth in the plan will be reduced or discontinued, pension costs should be accrued annually regardless of the funding arrangement, on the assumption that the company is a going concern and the plan is a long-term commitment. Pension plans, moreover, are an inherent part of the labor compensation structure and it is unreasonable to assume that a corporation as a going concern will terminate a pension plan even though it may reserve the right to do so.

4. *Uncertainties.* There are uncertainties surrounding the determination of pension costs such as employee turnover and mortality. Nevertheless, reasonable cost estimates can be made using actuarial techniques.

5. *Method of accrual.* The annual provision (and corresponding accrual) for pension cost should be in accordance with an accounting method that is related to an acceptable actuarial cost method. A number of such acceptable actuarial methods exist (but do not include terminal funding or pay-as-you-go) which have the desirable features that they are rational, systematic and can be consistently applied, so that the result is a reasonable and relatively stable charge to periodic income.

6. *Amount of annual provision.* The annual provision for pension cost should be determined on a consistent basis and should be no less than a minimum provision, and no more than a maximum, in accordance with the following description of such limits:

(a) *Minimum provision.* This is the total of (i) the normal cost, (ii) amount of interest on any unfunded prior service cost, and (iii) a provision for vested benefits, as explained below.

(b) *Maximum provision.* This is the total of (i) the normal cost, (ii) 10% of the past service (or prior service) cost, if any, and (iii) the amount of interest on the difference, if any, between periodic accrual of pension costs and the corresponding amounts funded.

(c) *Vested benefits.* Vested benefits are those payable to an employee whether or not he continues in the service of the employer even though the plan may provide that the amount payable be limited to the assets in the pension fund. As considered above in the computation of the minimum annual provision, a provision for vested benefits should be made if, in general, and subject to other computational factors set forth in APB Opinion No. 8, this amount, actuarially computed, exceeds the total of the pension fund and accruals.

7. *Actuarial gains and losses.* Such gains and losses should be spread over the current and future years using averaging or other techniques some of which may take into account past experience and future expectations. They may be applied to nomal cost and/or to past or prior service cost. Unrealized appreciation and depreciation (for example, of securities or other fund investments) should be recognized either in the basic actuarial assumptions or in computing actuarial gains and losses.

8. *Adjustment of prior-year costs.* If the company changes its method of accounting for pension cost, any adjustment of prior-year costs should be applied to the current and future years and should not be treated as a retroactive adjustment to retained earnings.

ADDITIONAL CPA ACCOUNTING THEORY EXAMINATION QUESTIONS AND SOLUTION GUIDES

GOODWILL

Question—May 1966 (2)

The Tiger Corporation, a retail fuel oil distributor, has increased its annual sales volume to a level three times greater than the annual sales of a dealer it purchased in 1958 in order to begin operations. The board of directors of Tiger Corporation recently received an offer to negotiate the sale of Tiger Corporation to a large competitor. As a result, the majority of the board wants to increase the stated value of goodwill on the balance sheet to reflect the larger sales volume developed through intensive promotion and the current market price of sales gallonage. However, a few of the board members would prefer to eliminate goodwill altogether from the balance sheet in order to prevent "possible misinterpretations." Goodwill was recorded properly in 1958.

(a) 1. Discuss the meaning of the term "goodwill." Do not discuss goodwill arising from consolidated statements or the conditions under which goodwill is recorded.

    2. List the techniques used to calculate the tentative value of goodwill in negotiations to purchase a going concern.

(b) Why are the book and market values of the goodwill of Tiger Corporation different?

(c) Discuss the propriety of: (1) Increasing the stated value of goodwill prior to the negotiations; and (2) Eliminating goodwill completely from the balance sheet prior to negotiations.

Solution Guide

(a) For a discussion of the meaning of goodwill, see solution to Question—May 1959 (4), page 97. The techniques for calculation are set forth on page 97.

(b) See solution to Question—May 1959 (4), page 97. The recorded goodwill was undoubtedly at cost, whereas the market value would only be considered in determining the selling price of the business as a whole.

(c) The principles pertaining to intangibles, their recording at cost and the basis of amortization and write-off are applicable; see discussion beginning on page 93.

THE MEANING OF GENERALLY ACCEPTED
ACCOUNTING PRINCIPLES

Question—May 1966 (3)

At the completion of the Darby Department Store audit, the president asks about the meaning of the phrase "in conformity with generally accepted accounting principles" that appears in your audit report on the management's financial statements. He observes that the meaning of the phrase must include more than what he thinks of as "principles."

(a) Explain the meaning of the term "accounting principles" as used in the audit report. (Do not discuss in this part the significance of "generally accepted.")

(b) The president wants to know how you determine whether or not an accounting principle is generally accepted. Discuss the sources of evidence for determining whether an accounting principle has substantial authoritative support. Do not merely list the titles of publications.

(c) The president believes that diversity in accounting practice always will exist among independent entities despite continual improvements in comparability. Discuss the arguments that support his belief.

Solution Guide

(a) See discussion beginning on page 50.
(b) See page 3.
(c) See page 133.

LONG-TERM LEASES

Question—May 1966 (7)

The practice of obtaining the right to use property by noncancelable leases is becoming more prevalent.

(a) Assets acquired under noncancellable leases that are in substance installment purchases should be capitalized in the accounts of the lessee in order to show the facts properly. List the defects in the lessee's balance sheet and income statement that would result from not recording assets acquired under such contracts.

(b) Other noncancellable leases that give the lessee essentially all the rights and obligations of ownership are not installment purchases in substance.

(i) Discuss the case against recording assets acquired by such leases.

(ii) The case for recording assets acquired by such leases rests primarily on the belief that the opportunity to exercise the right of use creates an asset that should be recognized in the accounts with its related liability. Discuss the arguments that *support* this belief.

Solution Guide

See section on long-term leases beginning on page 162, and on criteria for lease capitalization, page 164.

TIMING OF REVENUE RECOGNITION

Question—May 1965 (3c)

Revenue may also be recognized (1) during production and (2) when cash is received. For each of these two bases of timing revenue recognition, give an example of the circumstances in which it is properly used and discuss the accounting merits of its use in lieu of the sales basis.

Solution Guide

See discussion "Timing of Revenue Recognition," page 62.

TERMINOLOGY, DISCLOSURE AND CLASSIFICATION—
CRITICISM OF FINANCIAL STATEMENTS

Question—November 1964 (1)

The following year-end financial statements were prepared by the Colesar Corporation's bookkeeper. The Colesar Corporation operates a chain of retail stores.

BALANCE SHEET OF THE COLESAR CORPORATION

June 30, 1964

Assets

Current assets:		
Cash		$ 90,000
Notes receivable		100,000
Accounts receivable, less reserve for doubtful accounts		75,000
Inventories		395,500
Investment securities, at cost		100,000
Total current assets		760,500
Property, plant and equipment:		
Land, at cost (note 1)	$175,000	
Buildings, at cost less accumulated depreciation of $350,000	500,000	
Equipment, at cost less accumulated depreciation of $180,000	400,000	1,075,000
Intangibles		450,000
Other assets:		
Prepaid expenses		6,405
Total assets		$2,291,905

Liabilities and Owners' Equity

Current liabilities:		
Accounts payable		$ 25,500
Estimated income taxes payable		160,000
Contingent liability on discounted notes receivable		75,000
Total current liabilities		260,500
Long-term liabilities:		
5% serial bonds, $50,000 due annually on December 31		
Maturity value	$850,000	
Less amortized discount	35,000	815,000
Total liabilities		1,075,500

Owners' equity:
Common stock, stated value $10 (author-
ized and issued, 75,000 shares)   750,000
Retained earnings
Appropriated (note 2) $110,000
Free   356,405   466,405   1,216,405
    Total liabilities and owners' equity $2,291,905

INCOME STATEMENT OF THE COLESAR CORPORATION
June 30, 1964

Sales			$2,500,000
Interest income			6,000
Total revenue			2,506,000
Cost of goods sold			1,780,000
Gross margin			726,000
Operating expenses:			
Selling expenses			
Salaries	$95,000		
Advertising	85,000		
Sales returns and allowances	50,000	$230,000	
General and administrative expenses			
Salaries	84,000		
Property taxes	38,000		
Depreciation and amortization	86,000		
Rent (note 3)	75,000		
Interest on serial bonds	48,000	331,000	561,000
Net income before taxes			165,000
Provision for federal income taxes			160,000
Net income			$ 5,000

Notes to financial statements:

Note 1. Includes a future store site acquired during the year at a cost of $75,000.

Note 2. Retained earnings in the amount of $110,000 have been set aside to finance expansion.

Note 3. During the year the Company acquired certain equipment under a long-term lease.

Identify and discuss the defects in the preceding financial statements with respect to terminology, disclosure, and classification.
Your discussion should explain why you consider them to be defects.
Do not prepare revised statements. (You should assume that the
arithmetic is correct.)

Solution Guide

1. The term *reserve* should be used only to describe surplus reserves; the account should therefore have a name such as "allowance for doubtful accounts." (For further discussion regarding *reserves* see page 123.) There is also no disclosure regarding any charge to bad debts expense or the reason for any failure to make such a charge.

2. Inventories should be presented in the order of their liquidity as follows: finished goods, work in process, and raw materials. The basis of valuation of inventories should be stated and the method of costing should be disclosed.

3. Disclosure should be made of type of investments, and of their market value if they consist of marketable securities. Those securities that are considered to be truly current assets should be listed immediately following cash, although the "permanent" investments should be separately classified in a noncurrent section, usually immediately following the caption for total current assets.

4. The fixed asset section should include only land, buildings, plant, etc., used in operations; hence, the land held for future use should be separately classified in the noncurrent section rather than disclosed in the notes.

5. The nature of the intangibles and their basis of valuation should be disclosed. The income statement contains one figure for depreciation and amortization, but that portion representing amortization of intangibles should be separately disclosed.

6. Prepaid expenses should be shown as current assets. See discussion beginning on page 99.

7. The name of the account should be more fully expressed as "Estimated federal income taxes payable."

8. Notes receivable discounted should be shown not as a liability but as an offset against the notes receivable, with appropriate disclosure of the amount.

9. Current maturity of the serial bonds should be presented as a current liability.

10. Note 2 refers to retained earnings having been set aside. Since the phrase "set aside" is more properly used in connection with assets, the note should have used an expression such as "appropriation" or "reserve."

11. The income statement covers the year ended June 30, 1964.

12. Interest income is only incidental revenue unrelated to the regular operations of the business and should have been presented below,

possibly following operating income. A similar comment might be made regarding interest on serial bonds.

13. Sales returns and allowances should have been deducted from sales in arriving at revenue.

14. Note 3 regarding the long-term lease should be more informative; see page 165.

15. The provision for federal income taxes is almost 100% of the net income before taxes. This discrepancy should be explained; perhaps an income-tax allocation situation is involved requiring an allocation of an appropriate portion of the tax expense to perhaps retained earning as an offset to a gain reflected therein.

16. A statement of retained earnings should have been included.

CONTRIBUTED CAPITAL VERSUS EARNED CAPITAL

Question—November 1964 (3b)

The ownership interest in a corporation is customarily reported in the balance sheet as stockholders' equity. In the stockholders' equity section of the balance sheet a distinction is made between contributed capital and earned capital. Why is this distinction made? Discuss.

Solution Guide

See solution to Question—November 1959 (4), page 120.

"PROFITS OR LOSSES" ON TREASURY STOCK

Question—November 1964 (3c)

There is frequently a difference between the purchase price and the sale price of treasury stock, but accounting authorities agree that the purchase or sale of its own stock by a corporation cannot result in a profit or loss to the corporation. Why is the difference not recognized as a profit or loss to the corporation? Discuss.

Solution Guide

See discussion dealing with revenue and income beginning on page 57. Treasury stock is essentially the same as unissued stock. It is not an asset and, hence, does not yield revenue.

CASH FLOW STATEMENTS

Question—May 1964 (3)

A popular analytical tool employed by financial analysts and other readers of financial statements is the computation of the amount of cash flow. To provide more meaningful cash flow information that cannot be readily obtained from the balance sheet and the statement of income and retained earnings, it has been suggested that a funds statement be provided along with the other financial statements. The title of the funds statement should be descriptive, such as "Statement of Source and Application of Funds" or "Summary of Changes in Financial Position."

(a) Define the term cash flow from an accounting standpoint.

(b) Discuss each of the following statements:

(i) Cash flow provides a more significant indication of the results of a company's operations than does net income.

(ii) A large cash flow permits steady expansion and the regular payment of cash dividends.

(c) Discuss the uses to which funds statements may be put by the readers of the statements.

Solution Guide

See page 172 and discussion following.

CRITERIA FOR LEASE CAPITALIZATION

Question—November 1963 (2)

The practice of using long-term leases as a method of financing plant and equipment acquisitions is well established. In many cases these lease arrangements represent, in substance, a purchase of the property; therefore, the property and the obligations incurred should be reported among the assets and liabilities of the lessee.

(a) In the light of their combined effects upon the substance, rather than the form, of such arrangements, what provisions of a long-term lease contract would you consider as substantiating evidence that the lease involves the purchase of property?

(b) What is the effect on the financial statements (including the statement of sources and applications of funds) of recording the property and corresponding liabilities on the books of the lessee? Discuss.

Solution Guide

See page 162 and discussion following.

STOCK DIVIDENDS

Question—November 1963 (3)

The directors of Lenox Corporation are considering the issuance of a stock dividend. They have asked you to discuss the proposed action by answering the questions below.

(a) What is a stock dividend? How is a stock dividend distinguished from a stock split-up from a legal standpoint and from an accounting standpoint?

(b) For what reasons does a corporation usually declare a stock dividend? A stock split-up?

(c) Discuss the amount, if any, of retained earnings to be capitalized in connection with a stock dividend.

Solution Guide

(a,b) Both a stock dividend and a stock-split involve a corporation's issuance of additional shares of its common stock to its common stockholders without the receipt of any cash or property as consideration. In neither case is the corporation's net assets or stockholder's equity affected. As expressed in ARB No. 43, Chapter 7, the difference between the two arrangements depends principally on the relative size of the distribution, an issuance of additional shares of less than 20% or 25% of the previously outstanding shares being regarded as a stock dividend.

In the case of a stock dividend the intention is to distribute some evidence of a share in retained earnings without decreasing cash and affecting working capital. The purpose of a split-up is to effect a reduction in the unit market price of the shares, obtain a wider distribution, and improve the marketability of the stock.

From the legal standpoint, a stock dividend results in a transfer from retained earnings to contributed capital and, hence, an increase in "legal capital." A stock-split will simply affect the par or stated value of the capital stock.

(c) Retained earnings will usually be capitalized in an amount corresponding to the fair market value of the new shares issued. This amount corresponds to the value as a dividend ascribed to the stock by the stockholder. In a closely held company there is no need to capitalize retained earnings in excess of the par or stated value, which would be done simply to meet the legal requirements. This distinction in treatment rests on the ground that the shareholders of the publicly held corporation, because of dividend notices and public releases, look upon the distribution as equivalent to a cash dividend, whereas this is assumed not to be true for the stockholder in a closely held company.

ELEMENTS OF ACQUISITION COST

Question—November 1963 (7a)

Name the items in addition to the amount paid to the former owner or contractor that may be properly included as part of the acquisition cost of the following fixed assets: land, buildings, and machinery and equipment.

Solution Guide

See discussion, page 89.

PURPOSE OF ACCOUNTING PRINCIPLES

Question—May 1963 (7a)

For some time the need for the study and formulation of basic postulates and principles of accounting has been recognized. Discuss (1) the purpose of developing basic postulates and principles of accounting, and (2) the benefits to be derived from their development.

Solution Guide

See discussion beginning on page 1.

OBJECTIVITY

Question—May 1963 (7b,c)

Frequently advanced as a basic postulate is a general proposition dealing with "objectivity." Under what conditions, in general, is information arising from a financial transaction considered to be objective in nature?

Accountants acknowledge that financial statements reporting the results of operations for relatively short periods of time, say one year, are tentative whenever allocations between past, present, and future periods are required. On the other hand, the "objectivity" postulate leads to the logical deduction that changes in assets and liabilities, and the related effects (if any) on revenues, expenses, retained earnings, and the like should not be given formal recognition in the accounts earlier than the point of time at which they can be measured in objective terms. Can this apparent conflict be resolved? Discuss.

Solution Guide

See discussion beginning on page 18.

See sections "Certainty and Uncertainty," page 21 and "Dealing with Uncertainty," page 22.

INTERIM FINANCIAL STATEMENTS

Question—November 1962 (3)

Many corporations issue quarterly financial statements. In general the accounting concepts underlying these interim statements are the same as those underlying annual statements. However, certain concepts are modified in the development of interim statements because to treat the fiscal quarter as an independent accounting period might limit the usefulness of the interim statements to management, investors, and the public.

(a) On what matters does the knowledgeable reader attempt to draw conclusions from interim financial statements? (Assume the statements are reliable even though they are unaudited.)

(b) An objective of income presentation should be the avoidance of any practice that is adopted for the purpose of equalization of reported income. Discuss the modifications, if any, of this generally accepted principle that would be made in developing interim income statements with regard to sales, manufacturing costs including over- or underabsorbed overhead, and selling expenses including advertising.

Solution Guide

(a) See solution to Question—May 1964 (2), page 138. Some of these matters are: operating results, working capital position, trend, impact of seasonal factors, comparison with prior years for the given period, future prospects, and guide to results for the full year.

(b) In general, interim statements must similarly conform with generally accepted accounting principles. However, whereas annual statements may reflect the consistent policy of expensing such items as advertising expenses or under- or overabsorbed manufacturing burden, interim statements would show appropriate deferrals or accruals. The objective is to obviate the impact of factors that are purely accidental, seasonal, and irregular in terms of their occurrence within the given year. Accounts based upon factual events, such as sales, would certainly not be modified, although unusual variations or seasonal fluctuations might be disclosed.

DIRECT COSTING

Question—November 1962 (6a,b)

Supporters of direct costing have contended that it provides management with more useful accounting information. Critics of direct costing believe that its negative features outweigh its contributions. Describe direct costing. How does it differ from conventional absorption costing?

List the arguments for and against the use of direct costing.

Solution Guide

(a) See page 8. Direct costing is a technique by which manufacturing costs are divided between those which are fixed and those which vary directly with volume. Prime costs—direct material and direct labor—plus variable factory overhead are assigned to the product and thereby to inventory and cost of goods sold. Fixed manufacturing overhead costs are assigned to the period. Under conventional absorption costing, prime costs plus fixed and variable factory overhead are assigned to the product.

(b) The following concepts enter into the arguments for and against: managerial analysis; profit-volume analysis; usefulness for budgeting; overhead allocation problems; relevance or irrelevance of capacity costs; full cost as a generally accepted accounting principle; matching of full cost and revenue; distinction between fixed and variable costs; impact on income statement and balance sheet.

PURCHASE DISCOUNTS

Question—November 1962 (7b-1)

As generally presented in financial statements the item—cash discounts on purchases—has been criticized as improperly matching costs with revenues. Briefly discuss cash discounts on purchases from the viewpoint of matching costs with revenues and suggest corrected or alternative means of presenting the financial information.

Solution Guide

The following concepts are applicable: cost reduction; cash cost equivalent; no revenue upon acquisition of assets; financial income versus cost reduction; conservatism.

INVENTORY PRICING METHODS

Question—May 1962 (7)

Specific identification is sometimes said to be the ideal method for assigning cost to inventory and to cost of goods sold.

(a) List the arguments for and against the above statement.

(b) First-in, first-out; weighted average; and last-in, first-out methods are often used instead of specific identification. Compare each of these methods with the specific identification method. Include in your discussion an analysis of the theoretical propriety of each method in the determination of income and asset valuation. (Do not define the methods or describe their technical accounting procedures.)

Solution Guide

See page 83 for discussion of cost flow concepts. The following ideas are also applicable: balance sheet values; matching of cost and revenue; price-level changes; possibility of manipulation by expansion or contraction; emphasis on values rather than physical flow; replacement cost; consistency; income stabilization or equalization; practicability; availability of cost inventory records and other data; actual flow of physical merchandise; fictitious profits versus real income; relationship to taxes; impact on ratio and managerial analysis.

LOWER OF COST OR MARKET— CASE APPLICATIONS

Question—May 1961 (8a,b)

(a) In some instances, accounting principles require a departure from valuing inventories at cost alone. Determine the proper unit inventory price in the following cases:

	1	2	3	4	5
Cost	$2.00	$2.00	$2.00	$2.00	$2.00
Net realizable value	1.30	2.05	1.80	2.40	1.90
Net realizable value less normal profit	1.10	1.85	1.60	2.20	1.70
Market (replacement cost)	1.20	2.10	1.85	2.15	1.60

(b) Assume the item in Case 5 is also in stock at the end of the next fiscal period and the four values are respectively $2.00, $1.90, $1.70, and $2.05. What would be the proper unit price?

Solution Guide

(a) Under the lower of cost or market rule, the inventory would be valued at the lower of cost or replacement market, but replacement market should be no higher than the net realizable value and no lower than the net realizable value reduced by a normal profit margin.

Case 1. $1.20. The inventory is valued at replacement cost which is lower than cost.

Case 2. $2.00. The inventory is valued at cost which is lower than replacement cost.

Case 3. $1.80. The inventory is valued at net realizable value which is lower than both cost and replacement market.

Case 4. $2.00. The inventory is valued at cost which is lower than replacement market and net realizable value.

Case 5. $1.70. The inventory is valued at net realizable value reduced by a normal profit margin, because that figure is lower than cost but higher than replacement market.

(b) When an inventory is valued at an amount other than cost, under the lower of cost or market rule the assigned value becomes the new cost. Therefore, if the inventory in Case 5 were on hand at the end of the next fiscal year, it would be valued at $1.70, the new cost, which is lower than replacement market and net realizable value, the original cost of $2.00 being irrelevant.

REVENUE RECOGNITION

Question—November 1958 (2)

The generally accepted rule in accounting is that revenue is recognized when the sale is made.

(a) Why has the sale been chosen as the point at which to recognize the revenue resulting from the entire producing and selling process?

(b) What is the justification for the following deviations from recognizing revenue at the time of sale?

   (i) Installment sales method of recognizing revenue.

   (ii) Recognition of revenue during production in gold mining.

   (iii) The percentage-of-completion basis in long-term construction contracts.

Solution Guide

See solutions to Question—May 1965 (3), page 63, and Question—November 1965 (3), page 65.

PURCHASE VERSUS POOLING—A CASE SITUATION

Question—November 1960 (6c)

Prepare Wesco's journal entries from the following data to record the combination of Wesco, Southco and Eastco.

Effective December 31, 1959, Wesco Corporation proposes to acquire, in exchange for common stock, all of the assets and liabilities of Southco Corporation and Eastco Corporation, after which the latter two corporations will distribute the Wesco stock to their shareholders in complete liquidation and dissolution. Wesco proposes to increase its outstanding stock for purposes of these acquisitions. Balance sheets of each of the corporations immediately prior to merger on December 31, 1959 are given below. The assets are deemed to be worth their book values.

	Wesco	Southco	Eastco
Current assets	$ 2,000,000	$ 500,000	$ 25,000
Fixed assets (net)	10,000,000	4,000,000	200,000
Total	$12,000,000	$4,500,000	$225,000
Current liabilities	$ 1,000,000	$ 300,000	$ 20,000
Long term debt	3,000,000	1,000,000	105,000
Capital stock ($10 par)	3,000,000	1,000,000	50,000
Retained earnings	5,000,000	2,200,000	50,000
Total	$12,000,000	$4,500,000	$225,000
Other data relative to acquisition—			
Shares outstanding	300,000	100,000	5,000
Fair market value per share	$40	$40	$30
No. shares Wesco stock to be			
exchanged—for Southco assets		100,000	
for Eastco assets			5,000
Old management to continue?		Yes	No
Old shareholders to elect			
director on Wesco Board?		Yes	No

Solution Guide

Eastco (Purchase)

The following characteristics of the Wesco and Eastco combination indicate that it should be accounted for as a purchase: the elimination of Eastco's management; the inability of the stockholders of Eastco to elect a director on the Board of Wesco—hence they have no influence on the overall management; the relative size, the net assets of Eastco being less than 2% of the combined total of Wesco and Easto.

The following journal entry would be made on the books of Wesco to record the purchase of Eastco:

Current assets	$ 25,000	
Fixed assets	200,000	
Goodwill	100,000	
Current liabilities		$ 20,000
Long-term debt		105,000
Capital stock		50,000
Paid in surplus		150,000

To record the acquisition of Eastco in exchange for the issuance of 5,000 shares of $10 par value stock, market value $40 per share, in payment therefor.

The acquisition of Eastco is recorded on a cost basis, cost being measured by the fair value of the shares of Wesco given in exchange for the property of Eastco. The amount attributed to goodwill is the excess of the purchase price of $200,000 over the acquired net assets of Eastco which are accepted at book value. The amount assigned to goodwill could have been allocated to fixed and other assets if that portion of the purchase price is determined to be in fact attributable to those assets.

Southco (Pooling)

The business combination of Wesco with Southco reflects continuity of ownership and management and should be treated as a pooling of interests. The following journal entry should be made on the books of Wesco:

Current assets	$ 500,000	
Fixed assets	4,000,000	
Current liabilities		$ 300,000
Long-term debt		1,000,000
Capital stock		1,000,000
Retained earnings		2,200,000

To record a pooling of interests with Southco in exchange for the issuance of 100,000 shares of $10 par value stock, market value $40.

The assets, liabilities and retained earnings of Southco are carried over to the books of Wesco.

PENSION PLAN—STATEMENT DISCLOSURE

Question—November 1958 (7a)

Where the cost of such a pension plan is material, what disclosure should be given in the financial statements of the company for the year in which the plan is adopted?

Solution Guide

See page 174.

CAPITAL VERSUS REVENUE EXPENDITURES

Question—May 1958 (1)

Once equipment has been installed and placed in operation, subsequent expenditures relating to this equipment are frequently thought of as being in the nature of a repair or general maintenance, and hence chargeable to operations in the period in which the expenditure is made. Actually, determination of whether such an expenditure should be either charged to operations or capitalized involves a much more careful analysis of the character of the expenditure. What are the factors that should be considered in making such a decision? Discuss fully.

Solution Guide

See discussion beginning on page 90. In general, the following concepts are applicable: extension of useful life of asset; substantial improvement in efficiency; replacement of major parts; ordinary versus extraordinary; frequency of expenditure; materiality; consistency; character of property and the extent of identification of individual parts.

COST AND VALUE

Question—May 1958 (3)

The general manager of the Cumberland Manufacturing Company received an income statement from his controller. The statement covered the calendar year 1957. "Joe," he said to the controller, "this statement indicates that a net income of two million dollars was earned last year. You know the value of the company is not that much more than it was this time last year."

"You're probably right," replied the controller. "You see, there are factors in accounting which sometimes keep reported operating results from reflecting the change in the value of the company."

Prepare a detailed explanation of the accounting conventions to which the controller referred. Include justification, to the extent possible, for the generally used accounting methods.

Solution Guide

See discussion on "Utility and Asset Value" beginning on page 30 and on "Orientation," page 1.

CONCEPT OF DEPRECIATION

Question—November 1956 (2)

The chief engineer of a manufacturing firm suggested in a conference of the company's executives that the accountants should speed up depreciation on the machinery in Department 3 because "improvements are making those machines obsolete very rapidly, and we want to have a depreciation fund big enough to cover their replacement."

Discuss fully the accounting concept of depreciation and the effect on a business concern of the depreciation recorded for fixed assets, paying particular attention to the issues raised by the chief engineer.

Solution Guide

See discussion beginning on page 90.

CONSISTENCY AND CONSERVATISM

Question—May 1955 (1)

Inventories are often valued at the "lower of cost or market." This traditional method of valuation is frequently defended as "conservative" and, like any other valuation method adopted, should be followed consistently.

In your opinion, is a company which regularly follows the practice of valuing its inventory at the lower of cost or market being "consistent and conservative"? Discusss critically, including a discussion of the meaning of the terms *consistent* and *conservative*.

Solution Guide

See solutions to Question—May 1951 (5), page 37, Question—November 1958 (3a), page 43, and Question—November 1958 (3c), page 45.

DEPRECIATION METHODS

Question—May 1955 (7)

The Acme Manufacturing Company purchased a new machine that was especially built to perform one particular function on their assembly line. A difference of opinion has arisen as to the method of depreciation to be used in connection with this machine. Three proposals are now being considered by the president of the company:

(a) Depreciation based on the straight-line method.

(b) Depreciation based on the unit-of-production method.

(c) Depreciation based on the sum-of-the-years digits method.

List separately the arguments for and against each of the proposed methods from both the theoretical and practical viewpoints. In your answer, you need not express your preference and you are to disregard income tax consequences of all methods.

Solution Guide

See discussion beginning on page 90. The following concepts are also applicable: matching cost and revenue; directness of relationship to production; useful life; price-level; replacement cost; uncertainty regarding future benefits; obsolescence; conservatism; relationship to maintenance policy; grouping depreciation cost and maintenance expense to arrive at combined fixed asset cost; simplicity; record keeping; uncertainty regarding scrap value.

RESEARCH AND DEVELOPMENT COSTS

Question—May 1954 (7)

The Plastic Products Company maintains a research department. Research projects conducted during the accounting year 1953 were of the following types:
(a) For development of a new product.
(b) For improvement of a product presently being manufactured.
(c) For improvement of manufacturing methods.

Work on some of the projects was incomplete as of December 31, 1953. What considerations are involved in selecting the accounting treatment(s) of research costs to be used by Plastic Products Company? Discuss fully, including discussion of the various ways in which the research costs may be presented in the financial statements.

Solution Guide

See discussion beginning on page 101.

INSTALLMENT BASIS OF ACCOUNTING

Question—May 1952 (5)

The Jones Co. sells furniture on the installment plan. For its Federal income tax returns, it reports its profit from sales on the installment basis. For its financial reports, it considers the entire profit to be earned in the year of sale.
(a) Discuss the relative merits of the two methods of reporting income.
(b) Explain the installment basis as used for income tax purposes.
(c) Discuss the effects of the use of these two bases by the Jones Co. on the significance of its reported annual income.

Solution Guide

See solutions to Question—May 1965 (3a,b), page 63, and Question—November 1965 (3a), page 65.

LOWER OF COST OR MARKET

Question—November 1951 (1)

In selecting a basis for pricing inventories, accountants have as one important objective the proper determination of income by matching appropriate cost against revenue. Does the pricing of inventories at "cost or market, whichever is lower" conflict with that objective? Discuss fully, including consideration of the effect of the "cost or market" rule on the usefulness of income statements and balance sheets.

Solution Guide

See discussion beginning on page 81.

PURPOSE AND LIMITATIONS OF
FINANCIAL STATEMENTS

Question—May 1951 (8)

The published report of a corporation was criticized because it was claimed that the income statement does not by any means give a clear picture of annual earning power and that the balance sheet does not disclose the true value of the fixed assets.

Considering the criticism made, you are to prepare an explanation of the nature and purpose of the income statement and of the balance sheet, including an explanation of their limitations.

Solution Guide

See discussion beginning on page 4.

INVENTORY VALUATION ABOVE COST

Question—November 1948 (6b)

State and illustrate under what conditions, if ever, it is considered proper to state inventories regularly above cost.

Solution Guide

See page 86 for listed conditions.

INDEX